HOW TO WRITE A
WINNING BUSINESS PLAN

A STEP-BY-STEP GUIDE FOR STARTUP
ENTREPRENEURS TO BUILD A SOLID
FOUNDATION, ATTRACT INVESTORS AND ACHIEVE
SUCCESS WITH A BULLETPROOF BUSINESS PLAN

WALTER GRANT

CONTENTS

INTRODUCTION

"Good business leaders create a vision, articulate the vision, passionately own the vision, and relentlessly drive it to completion."
— Jack Welch

Are you aware that 90% of startups fail? Of the few businesses that manage to get venture capital, which is a testament to great product ideas, 75% fail within the first five years. Starting a new business requires more than just a good product idea. Being part of the 10% that does make it requires you, as an entrepreneur, to have a vision that is well articulated and relentlessly pursued. In short, it requires a business plan.

The top reasons why most business startups fail include a lack of focus, a lack of domain-specific business knowledge crucial for the business to succeed in the ever-competitive environment, and a lack of a good business strategy. Rushing to invest money without addressing these fundamentals, as the statistics above show, does not guarantee success. Any business idea, if properly groomed before being deployed, has the potential to be part of the 10% and grow to be a multi-million-dollar company.

Are you thinking of starting a business? The first step that will propel you toward success is to focus on creating and articulating your vision by creating a business plan. In the process, you will rediscover and magnify the passion for the vision, which will give you the momentum you need to drive the vision to completion. But where do you start? Can you make a business plan on your own or do you need a consultant? What are the components of a business plan? How do you succeed in making and presenting a bulletproof business plan that people will understand?

This book is a step-by-step guide that will help you answer all these questions. It will also help you become more confident in the process of making a solid and well-structured business plan. This book will answer all the questions above and help you understand the importance and benefits of making a business plan.

The book starts by introducing the business model canvas, which is a strategic management tool that will enable you to understand, visualize, and create a business model in a structured and simple manner using known building blocks. Each of the nine chapters that follow will tackle the nine essential blocks that make up a business plan. By the time you are done, not only will you have a complete business plan, but your mindset and approach to business will be completely different.

Written by an entrepreneur at heart, this book is a gem that will help you learn from someone who has been in the trenches over and over again and has come out victorious. Walter Grant always has his hands on the newest trends regarding business development and is eager to share his experience with other entrepreneurs.

Do you want to start a successful business? Even with a shoestring budget, all you need to open the door to success is a well-written business plan. Turn the page, and discover the step-by-step guide to creating a business plan to get you the results you want.

CHAPTER 1: WHAT IS THE BUSINESS MODEL CANVAS AND WHY IS IT IMPORTANT FOR BUSINESS?

Customers demand products and services that, in their opinion, have value. Those in business have to figure out how to profitably create and deliver this value in the form of products. A key issue to figure out in the early stages of developing a business idea is how a business can create value for itself while delivering products and services that are valuable to its customer. The business model seeks to answer that question. It determines if a business has fully planned its road map and if it will eventually take off, survive, and thrive in an environment fraught with competition.

THE BUSINESS CREATION JOURNEY

To put this in perspective, picture someone who is going on a journey. If the person knows where they are going but has no idea how to get there and does not have a map, the journey will be long and winding. A business plan forces an entrepreneur to map out the route and the resources they will need to make it to the set destination. It also gives the entrepreneur a chance to step back, assess the chosen routes, and compare them with alternatives. This way, the best-case scenario will be chosen, taking into account the following:

- **The feasibility of the journey.** Sometimes, one can get so caught up in the excitement of starting something new that they forget to check if the idea is realistic. If to get to the destination, you need to come up with antics that only a person with superpowers can perform, then it might not be worth it to embark on the journey at all! Instead, it might be better to spend time looking for alternative routes that are more accessible.
- **The shortest path to the goal.** Incubating an idea for too long leaves you open to

obsolescence. The business world is fast-moving. Some business opportunities have windows that open briefly. These quickly get snapped up by nimble entrepreneurs who are quick on their feet. If you are always too late to the party because your planning process takes forever, you won't enjoy as much success as those around you.

- **Alternative routes.** There are always some unexpected curveballs that one encounters on their journey to success. Should this happen, if you have alternate routes already in mind, you won't waste time fumbling for solutions.

- **Stumbling blocks.** Many factors make it difficult for entrepreneurs to successfully implement business ideas. Examples include legal requirements, patent restraints, and competitors. It is easiest to tackle something that has been anticipated and carefully planned for.

- **Resources required on the journey.** These may be financial resources, human resources, physical resources, or industry know-how. Without adequate resources, you won't make it to your destination.

- **Cost.** The ideal path should be the cheapest but most efficient method to achieve the same goal. This way, more value will be created for the company.
- **The key.** If you get to your destination and cannot unlock the door, you cannot possibly say you have completed your mission. The key in business is understanding exactly what the customer wants. Sure, you might have a good product idea. But if it is not what the customer wants, or if it is not packaged the right way, you will waste a lot of time trying to figure out how to convert this product into revenue. If you plan properly before you embark on your journey, you will take this key with you and keep it safe to ensure it doesn't get lost along the journey.

The following section defines key terms that will be used throughout this book. These definitions will ensure there is no ambiguity between their usage in this book and their interpretation by the reader.

Business model: This is a plan designed to ensure the successful operation of a business. At the bare minimum, this plan should cover the following aspects that are fundamental to the success of any business: value propositions, key resources, key activities, key partners, cost structure, targeted customer segments, customer relationships, channels, and revenue streams.

Business model canvas: This is a strategic management tool that enables the entrepreneur to understand, visualize, and create a business model in a structured and simple manner using the nine building blocks identified above.

Product: This is a good or service that a business intends to sell to its customers. In this book, the term 'product' represents both tangible and intangible forms and encompasses ideas, physical goods, services, or a combination of the three. As such, instead of using the term 'goods' and/or 'services,' the book will refer to 'products.'

Stakeholders: These are groups of people who have an interest in a business enterprise. All these stakeholders should be consulted and/or included when creating a business plan.

Examples of these are:

- Owners of the business in their various capacities,
- Financiers,
- Central and local government departments whose jurisdiction can enable or constrain the takeoff of the business,
- Customers who make up the target market for the products,
- Suppliers,
- Competitors,
- And business consultants.

WHAT IS A BUSINESS MODEL?

Barring philanthropic business ventures, the main reason for creating a business is to make a profit. This only happens when a business can create value for itself in the process of creating value for its shareholders. A business model zooms in on this value creation objective and takes a wider perspective by bringing to the fore the following:

- How a business creates value
- How this value is delivered
- How value is then captured by the business

Value creation is the basis or foundation on which all businesses are formed. Value is created under these three conditions (Jorgenson, 2020):

1. **Irreversibility:** All value-creating economic transformations and transactions are thermodynamically irreversible. This means the impact of your product will have an impact on your target audience, and the customer experience will not be the same again without your product.
2. **Reduced entropy:** The Oxford Dictionary defines entropy as the level of disorder in a system. All value-creating economic transformations and transactions reduce disorder within the economic system and provide smarter, effective, and more efficient ways of doing things.
3. **Usefulness:** All value-creating economic transformations and transactions produce products that are useful to the target group. It is this usefulness that will ultimately make the customer purchase the product.

That said, to create value, the business idea should be solid enough to endure prodding tests that include the following:

Does the business idea solve a problem? A solution to a problem is what determines the attractiveness of a product. As you are brainstorming for your business plan, ask yourself the following questions:

- What are customers going to use this product for?
- Why is it useful?
- How will it help in solving any existing issues?
- What gap is the product filling in the market?
- In what way is this product better than the existing products in solving these issues?

Will people pay for the product? This is the only way that a business idea can be validated as capable of creating value for its intended customer base. If people are willing to pay, how much are they willing to pay for the product? This question forces the entrepreneur to step back from entrepreneur bias. If your head is stuck in the allure of coming up with a great product idea and seeing it come alive, you will be tempted to value the product in terms of the effort you have put into the project. However, if you put on the customers' shoes and look at what the product is worth from their perspective, you will be forced to be more analytic and astute in your approach to business.

Is the product capable of generating value for the business? Value is created in the path that the product goes through from product idea generation to product development to delivery. For value to be created, the price that customers are willing to pay should be below the cost incurred by the company to develop and deliver the product. The most successful entrepreneurs are those who can innovatively discover the least expensive methods to solve existing problems in a scalable way.

How substitutable is the product? The key is to aim to be unique in one way or the other. If the idea is not differentiated enough from the other numerous products on the market, what will make the customers sit up and notice the product? In other words, if your being in or out of business makes no difference at all to the customers as other businesses with the same undifferentiated product will simply take your place, you won't be able to create much value for the company.

Is there a sizable market for the product? The market refers to the customer base that the business is likely to attract with its product offering. If the market base is sizable, the business has better chances of succeeding. Markets that appear to have a potentially non-scalable customer base should be approached with caution.

CREATING A BUSINESS PLAN

As discussed above, a business model is a clear roadmap that details where the business is now, what it intends to achieve, and how it will meet these objectives. The effort applied in coming up with this business plan varies among entrepreneurs. There are two types of entrepreneurs in business: the risk-seeking entrepreneur and the cautious entrepreneur

The Risk-Seeking Entrepreneur

The first group comprises entrepreneurs who choose to just wing it in business. They mainly rely on their gut feeling to decide whether or not to jump into something. A little preliminary research is all they need, and if they feel they are onto something, they do not hesitate, instead, jumping in with both feet. By and large, this group is likely cash-rich, which means that they are not resource-constrained. They, therefore, have the flexibility to invest large sums of money in any project they feel has potential. They are also risk seekers and understand that with risk comes the probability of loss. As such, if a business venture is a flop, they are likely to just shrug it off and move on to the next potential business idea until they strike gold. Understandably, because they are not resource-constrained, this is not the typical entrepreneur who you are likely to encounter in normal day-to-day business.

The Cautious Entrepreneur

This is the typical entrepreneur to whom a business is not something that one just rushes into half-blind. Meticulous and detailed work goes into under-standing all aspects that are likely to make the business venture a success. Decisions made are based on data and facts collated from studying the market. Any extrapolated trends used as a basis for decision-making can be explained and backed using statistical information and data gathered through market research. A business venture is treated as a multi-stakeholder decision that should be approached with caution if value is to be created.

A business plan is thus a platform that all stakeholders involved in the business venture can refer to for guidance regarding common objectives and strategies fashioned to attain these objectives. With this cautious approach, chances of failure are minimized. Each business venture undertaken is a calculated move that has been analyzed from various angles and has a high probability of success.

Given the importance of a business plan, how do you condense everything discussed above and still come up with a clear roadmap that not only makes sense to you but to all stakeholders who want to understand your business venture?

THE BUSINESS MODEL CANVAS AS AN IMPORTANT BUSINESS TOOL

The business model canvas is a strategic management tool that enables you to understand, visualize, and create a business model in a structured and simple manner using known building blocks. The blocks on the canvas include the following:

Customer segments: These are the target customers who are likely to see value in the business's products. Research on this block should identify the following:

- Who the customers are and the most important audience for the company
- What the customers consider to be valuable about the product
- The various ways in which the customers can be segmented or stratified
- How customers feel about the product.
- How the customers are currently going about satisfying the solution that the product will solve

Value propositions: A value proposition is a clear statement that describes why stakeholders should engage in business with the entrepreneur. For this statement to be unambiguous, the business model should clearly state how the business is going to do the following:

- Create value through its product offering
- Attract customers to the product
- Get customers to choose that product over competitors' products

Channels: These are the different ways that the product will be promoted, sold, and delivered to the target market. This block should include a justification of these particular channels and an analysis of whether the channels are likely to work as intended. Questions to be answered include:

- Which distribution channels work best for the business?
- Are these channels congruent with the channels preferred by the customers?
- What are the cost implications of these distribution channels?
- How best can these channels be integrated into both the business and customers' routines?

Customer relationships: These are the different ways that you can use to interact with potential customers. This includes strategies to attract these customers to your product, convince them to try the product, convert them into loyal customers, and grow the customer base. Forging a relationship between customers and the business takes effort and money. If done right, customer relations should affect the structure of the business. Customer relationships, including the implications thereof, should be considered, nurtured, tended to, and integrated into the business plan right from the start. The success of the business depends on the strength of the relationship it has with its customers.

Revenue streams: This is an analysis of how the business is likely to earn revenues from its value proposition. This analysis is meant to align your expected revenue streams with those of your targeted customer base. Questions that will aid this analysis include:

- What values are the customers willing to pay for?
- What are they currently paying for a similar product?
- How much do they prefer to pay?
- When collated, what's the overall contribution of all the revenue streams to the business?

Key resources: These are the strategic resources and assets the business needs to create and deliver value to its target customers. Resources can be classified into the following categories:

- Physical resources
- Intellectual resources
- Human resources
- Financial resources

Key activities: From the value propositions, you should synthesize the key activities you need to engage in to create the product, promote it, and deliver it to the customers. Key activities require an analysis of the production process, distribution channels, customer relationships, and revenue streams.

Key partnerships: This is essentially a stakeholder analysis. The business plan should identify which stakeholders you need to work with to make the business a success and what their motivations are.

Cost structure: This block identifies the major cost drivers in the business. This analysis should identify the most important costs and the most expensive key resources and activities.

THE GRAPHICAL PRESENTATION OF THE BUSINESS MODEL

Key partners	Key activities	Value propositions	Customer relationships	Customer segments
What can the company outsource to deliver its value propositions efficiently?	What strategic things does the business do to deliver its propositions?	Why would customers choose this product over that of competitors?	How will the business interact with the customers to create and maintain a relationship?	Who are the customers?
	Key resources		**Channels**	
	What unique strategic assets must the business have to deliver its value propositions?		How does the customer get the product and the value propositions?	
Cost structure		**Revenue streams**		
What are the business's major cost drivers?		How does the business earn revenue from the value propositions?		

Source: Enterprising Oxford (n.d.)

WHY USE THE BUSINESS MODEL CANVAS?

Creating a business model is not an overnight activity. It involves effort from several team members and research gathered from various sources over time. If not done properly, the model can become wieldy and complex, making it difficult to navigate. It is not easy to comb through and understand a business model that has hundreds of pages.

The use of the business model canvas takes care of these issues and yields the following advantages:

1. **Easy to understand.** This tool enables you to synthesize and present all the information collected on a single page. As such, it is a visual tool that enables you to present all the aspects of the business plan in a concise and easy-to-understand manner.

2. **Focused.** Synthesizing multiple pieces of information and compressing all the important details to fit on a single page removes fluff. Only the most important issues are brought to the fore, which makes the business plan a very lean, focused, and useful tool.

3. **Easily malleable.** Since it is a single-page document, it is very easy to quickly present different ideas and analyze the impact of these changes on the business.

4. **Customer-focused.** The customer base that a business has is what makes or breaks the business. The model forces you to focus on the customer and to model everything around the customer by looking at the following:

- The value the business will provide to the customer

- If this value is in line with customer expectations
- What it takes to deliver this value

This customer-centric approach ensures that the business designs and delivers to the market a product tailored to suit the needs of the customer. An advantage that directly flows from this is guaranteed demand for the product.

1. **Shows interrelations between building blocks.** The graphical nature of the canvas shows how the different parts of the models are related and work together to deliver value. It is easy to visualize the impact of changes in one block on the other aspects of the model and how these will eventually affect value generation for the business as a whole.

2. **Easy to explain to other stakeholders.** With the canvas, there is no need to plow through lots of pages and fumble for the best way to explain how your business model is best set up to create and deliver value. It is designed to have all the talking points on one page. It is easy to convince other stakeholders to get

on board and share the same vision by focusing on how the key drivers of the business fit together unambiguously.

HOW TO USE THE BUSINESS MODEL CANVAS AS PART OF YOUR DAILY ROUTINE

When developing a business idea, an important objective for any business is survival. Survival only occurs if the business can make enough money to cover all its costs. From the first day when a business idea is conceived, the expectation is that the entrepreneur starts scanning the environment looking for signs that show that the idea is profitable and worth the risk. The information gathered through this process will not follow a straightfor-ward pattern and will come from different sources, some of which may be unexpected. How do you keep track of all this information as part of your daily routine? As new ideas are bounced around daily, all of which is a normal process of sharpening a business idea, how do you ensure that all leads are noted and given adequate research? Daily, you will also need to answer the following questions in no particular order:

- Which partners do I need to work with to make this business proposal feasible?
- Is the business equipped to carry out all the key activities involved?
- What key resources and infrastructure does the business need to take off?
- What value proposition will differentiate the product from that of competitors?
- Who are the customers that are likely to be interested in the product?
- What channels should be developed and used for the product to efficiently deliver the identified value propositions?
- How will the business attract the target customers and convince them to try the product?
- What is the cost structure of the business?
- What revenue streams are likely to be realized?

Each of these questions has to be tackled, and depending on how the business is organized, this might be happening daily as part of refining the business plan. Since the business environment is not static, this is a continuous process that will continue long after the business has taken off. The business model canvas provides a structured way to present all this information and will bring a much-appreciated order to your daily routine.

Creating a business model is a process that is fuzzy for most entrepreneurs, but with the business model canvas, all the above questions are answered in the most comprehensive manner possible. The result of using a business model canvas is an effective business strategy that will determine the following:

1. How the business will create, deliver and maintain its key values
2. How the business venture will be financed
3. How the business will differentiate itself from competitors
4. How well the business will be able to adjust to change in business conditions

Each of the following chapters will target one building block from the business model canvas. In each chapter, the building block will be looked at in-depth, helping you understand how each block fits into the business plan. To top it off, the Google company will be used as an example of how to build a business model canvas.

CHAPTER 2: KEY PARTNERS

Business involves taking on risk in return for a reward. Starting a business venture does not mean that the owners are guaranteed a 100% probability of succeeding. By investing money in this venture, depending on how the business model is structured, the business owner is choosing to brave several business risks. As part of managing risk exposure, it is ideal that a business focuses on a small aspect in the value chain where it has a comparative advantage. This requires an understanding of the business ecosystem and comparative advantages therein and how this knowledge can be used to choose key partners.

THE BUSINESS ECOSYSTEM

The business ecosystem is the network of organizations that are involved in the delivery of a product (Hayes, 2019). This implies that while still mulling a business idea, research aimed at understanding the process chain and all the organizations that are involved from the production to the delivery of the product to the customer should be undertaken. In any business ecosystem, typical organizations include:

- Suppliers
- Distributors
- Competitors
- Government agencies
- Customers

Understanding the ecosystem means that you can identify barriers to entry. It also means that as a new entrant into the market, you have to fight to create a spot for yourself within this ecosystem and start developing relations with other entities.

To understand how important knowledge of the ecosystem is, think of someone who has come up with a low-cost housing model targeted at the low-income group. To make this product affordable, the entrepreneur intends to use alternative building materials that are cheaper than the standard brick and mortar. In the model, the business is going to be the developer. The plan is to purchase land and then construct low-cost housing that will be affordable to the target group. The entrepreneur is confident that the use of the alternative materials will lower the production cost allowing for good profit margins.

ASSESSMENT OF A BUSINESS IDEA AND CHOICE OF KEY PARTNERS

This business mentioned previously can only take off if key partners are chosen carefully. Statistics show that there is a need for between 7.2 and 12 million units of affordable housing units in the United States (Ulman, 2020). There is clearly a market for this type of product. However, the low-income housing space is a sector that has a lot of stakeholders, including the following:

Government: Before the business idea can take off, there is a need for government buy-in in the form of development permits and compliance with all central and local authority regulations. The alternative materials have to be tested and approved, and the model plans can only be used if they meet specified health standards as listed in building bylaws. It might also not be possible to source for land from the open market as it has to be land that complies with zoning laws. In some areas, land for low-income housing can only be procured from the local authority.

Financiers: Even though the housing shortage statistic figures suggest that there is a huge demand for low-income housing, the target group is unlikely to have the financial means to purchase these houses without financial aid. As such, the business model can only realize the projected profits if financial partners are secured to provide long-term mortgage finance to the target group. These could be the government if it can provide subsidies to the target group, non-governmental organizations, and/or private financiers such as building societies or commercial banks that are willing to offer subsidized interest rates. Without this financial aid, the target group is unlikely to qualify for mortgage finance.

Raw material suppliers: There are a lot of materials that go into housing construction that will need to be supplied by other businesses that have a comparative advantage in that area, including cement and bricks for the foundation, nails, materials for the superstructure, roofing materials, water pipes, tubing, and electrical wires.

Infrastructure and services: These are facilities that are an essential component of any residential development to make it habitable. Examples of infrastructure needed in any residential development are:

- Transport infrastructure: Local road networks that are connected to the existing road network, footpaths and cycleways, public transport
- Waste management: Waste collection, recycling services
- Utilities: Water supply, sewer systems, electricity and gas network, telecommunications
- Health infrastructure: Local clinics, hospitals
- Education facilities
- Community infrastructures: Libraries, swimming pools
- Retail: Grocery stores, banks, restaurants

As can be seen in this example, the successful development and delivery of habitable residential housing require multiple stakeholders. All the businesses and organizations that have to work together to make housing delivery possible form the ecosystem. Within this ecosystem, entities affect each other and are also affected by the economic environment. For example, if due to an increase in construction activity in the economy in general, there is a high demand for cement and other general construction materials, prices may go up. If cement is a major raw material in the model, then estimated profit margins at the estimated affordable price may not be realized. Increasing the price to cover the increase in the cost of inputs may mean that the housing is no longer affordable to the targeted low-income group.

To survive, each business within the ecosystem has to be flexible enough to adapt to change. One way to do this is to assess how vulnerable you are as a firm and to identify key partners that you can work with so that as a business, you only focus on doing what you know best—the construction of the housing units.

How vulnerable are you as a firm? If you have assessed your vulnerabilities, it is then possible to model your business by choosing key partners that can help limit adverse impacts to the identified vulnerabilities. For example, if your suppliers are prone to stock-outs, you are better off using a stock management system that ensures you have a significant lead time to tide you over and insulate you from stock-outs.

Comparative advantages: Comparative advantages exist if a company can produce a product at a lower cost compared to its competitors. This could be attributable to previous significant investment in the following areas:

1. **Research and development.** This may have yielded knowledge and techniques that other firms do not have. Some companies have comparative advantages due to economies of scale. Key partners will then be used to access materials in areas where the business has no comparative advantage.
2. **Economies of scale.** These are cost savings that arise from efficiency in the production process. If a business has economies of scale, as the volume of production goes up, the average cost of producing the product goes down. The ability to realize these economies

of scale by producing more of a product, however, is determined by both internal and external factors.

- Internal factors that bring down production costs include the ability to purchase inputs in bulk, which results in lower input costs, better bargaining power than competitors, and possessing specialized inputs (e.g. specialized labor and machinery production processes).
- External factors that bring down production costs include industry growth, lower employment costs, industry infrastructure to support growth, and improved technology.

WHAT NON-KEY ACTIVITIES CAN YOU OUTSOURCE?

The residential housing development business idea described above will only be a success if it meets all regulatory health and safety standards and is attractive enough for the target group to want to live there. Anything substandard may not attract the expected number of customers and may also have undesirable repressions and costs in the process of fixing any identified issues. There is no way the new business can undertake to provide everything that is needed to make residential development a success. To proceed with the business idea, it becomes paramount that there be key partners who will be engaged to provide all the other infrastructure and services to make the project a success.

Outsourcing is part of strategic management. If done properly, it increases the chances of success, and the business will be able to generate more value. The following are the non-key activities that a business can outsource:

Key Activities Where You Do Not Have a Comparative Advantage

In the pursuit of delivering a quality product at the lowest cost possible, a business may have to consider how to best deliver different aspects or services tied to the product. In most cases, some of these services require that the business dabbles in areas where it doesn't have any comparative advantages. Examples where this may happen are given below:

Uber

One of Uber's value propositions is to give customers a ride when they need it. However, to provide these rides, they do not have the resources and the infrastructure necessary to buy, maintain, and manage thousands of vehicles and drivers spread throughout over 600 cities across the 65 countries where Uber is operational. It, therefore, follows that the key partners for Uber are the people who own cars and have time to drive using the Uber app. Without these drivers, Uber cannot deliver on its value proposition.

Electric Vehicle Manufacturer

A company that is venturing into the production of electric vehicles will need charging points for this model to work. A lack of easily accessible public charging power points can dampen demand for electric vehicles. To create effective demand for electric vehicles requires getting on board different stakeholders who will work together to provide this essential service. The company engaging in electric car manufacturing may not be able to do this effectively as charging infrastructure is capital intensive and requires large investments upfront. Capital constraints may make it impossible for the startup to fund both electric vehicle car manufacturing and provision of charging points. Key partners who can make this possible, however, are:

- Location owners who have the land and space that can be used to install the charging systems.
- Charge point operators who will install and manage electric charging points in various locations. This business will be responsible for maintenance, price setting, and data management.
- Power suppliers who will make available the required electricity.

Residential Housing Construction

In the example given above, constructing a super-structure requires a host of other skills that the business may not be able to efficiently provide. Trying to do so in-house may either compromise quality or result in the cost being astronomical. Examples are the plumbing, electrical wiring, and roofing. Outsourcing roofing, for example, means hiring a company that has been in the business for a long time and has access to the following:

- Ability to buy roof supplies in bulk if they have lots of customers. This will result in a lower cost due to economies of scale.
- Skilled workmen who have perfected the art

over the years and can produce high-quality workmanship.

- Access to lots of equipment that is specific to roofing.

Routine and Time-Consuming Tasks

These are tasks that can be easily done by anyone as long as they understand what exactly needs to be done. As an entrepreneur, you have to appreciate that time is money. Even though you might have the skill to do all the activities, you are better off spending most of your time on skill-demanding activities that cannot be efficiently done by anyone else and will earn you more money. Examples of these routine and time-consuming tasks are:

Research-related tasks: In the early phase of idea development and test marketing, there is a lot of research that needs to be done. Research may involve analyzing market trends, surveying target customers, data entry, coding, cleaning, and analysis. This is one small part of all the research that the business needs to undertake. As a small business that is starting, it is unlikely that there will be a dedicated research team under full-time employment. Attempting to do all these activities internally may mean that the research will take longer to be completed, and while this is being done, all the key personnel will not be available to carry out the other critical activities that will generate value for the business.

Receptionist and secretarial tasks: These tasks include answering the phone, taking down messages, screening calls, responding to emails, taking notes in meetings, and transcribing.

Services Where Employees Do Not Have the Requisite Skills

Most businesses start small with only core staff who are skilled at producing the prototype that forms the basis of testing the value creation capabilities of the product. Facebook, Google, YouTube, Mattel, and many other multi-billion-dollar companies started in garages or apartments with only a handful of employees who were passionate about the product and directly involved in its creation. However, for a business to take off, there is a need for other key services that the employees may not be skilled at. When it becomes necessary for an aspiring entrepreneur on their journey to success to don different hats and perform these other services even if they are not trained or skilled, there are two options:

- The first option is to try and do everything in-house, which will require that employees juggle their core tasks with these other services.
- The second option is to outsource.

The pros and cons of these two options will be fully explored in the next section. However, attempting to do everything in-house to save a few dollars has a lot of invisible costs that are best avoided such as lost time and a shoddy job. Examples of services that are best outsourced are marketing services, digital platforms, and accounting services as explained below:

Marketing Services

Marketing for startups is what gives the fledgling business a boost that can make a difference between success and failure. If the business is not known, and customers are not aware of the novel and revolutionary product that will solve some of their problems, then the journey to success will be longer. That said, it is best to outsource the marketing function to a professional, leaving the core employees to focus on the key in-house activities that will improve the value-creating capabilities of the product. The following advantages accrue to the business if marketing is done right:

It creates product awareness. If people are aware of the unique value propositions that your product has to offer, your product is likely to get a higher number of innovators, which will smooth the process of consumer adoption. The consumer adoption process has five stages:

- Product awareness
- Product interest
- Product evaluation
- Product trial
- Product adoption

Acknowledge right from the start that product innovation is not just about the ingeniousness of the technology behind the product. It is also about getting customers onboard and creating those revenue streams that will result in value creation for the business. There is, as a result, a huge aspect of business operations that is psycho-social and should not be taken lightly if a business venture is to succeed.

Before an innovative product is adopted, consumer resistance must be understood and overcome. Active and passive initial resistance, active and passive emergent resistance, belated resistance, and group resistance are examples of some terms that may not need an explanation to a professional marketer. These issues determine the marketing strategy undertaken to overcome resistance and fast-track the consumer adoption process. However, if this marketing function is not taken seriously and left to an employee whose hands are already full with other key duties that are essential for the product to be rolled out on time, the product might not do so well on the market.

A marketing strategy should not be treated as an afterthought when coming up with a business model. Since a marketing strategy is pivotal to the success of the business, it should be created early on to do the following:

- Conduct market research to determine and preempt possible hurdles that the company might encounter in the marketplace.
- Work together with the product development team to refine and tweak the product to come up with a more relevant

product positioned to appeal to the target group.

- Come up with a marketing plan that is best aligned to the goals of the business. This includes driving communication and product awareness and arranging for product trials and product launches.
- Working with the sales teams to create and develop leads and then convert these into sales.
- Ensure that customers who purchase the product are retained.

Digital Platforms

Digital platforms are a collection of tools that a company uses to create value by facilitating transactions. Going digital opens up markets and enables the business to compete with ease on multiple platforms. The advent of the internet, automation, and artificial intelligence have revolutionized the way that business is done. To move with the times, new businesses have to integrate these innovations into their business operations.

It is not realistic to expect an employee who does not know HTML, CSS, JQUERY, .NET, or the necessary programming language to create a website that is fully functional and will provide the best customer service experience. An attempt to do this in-house with inexperienced staff will lead to frustration, a lot of wasted time that could have been used elsewhere, less productivity, and shoddy work. As such, instead of doing this in-house, it might be best to outsource the creation of and maintenance of such digital tools.

Accounting Services

Accounting is a technical field that requires specialized skills and experience. For most businesses, accounting is not a core competency, and the initial staff may not have the technical know-how to prepare all the books of accounts. Hiring a professional firm to do your books means access to a team of professionals who have experience from working with other businesses in your field. The firm can also offer support, invaluable advice, and access to resources to support the decision-making process.

For a startup, accounting services are essential for the following;

- Creating financial forecasts that aid in the development of business plans.

- Understanding cash flow patterns and other key business metrics essential for decision-making.
- Providing data that can help you evaluate the impact of investments on revenues and cash flow patterns.
- Maintaining up-to-date bookkeeping records that can be used to seek venture capital.
- Receiving financial advice that will steer the company toward success.
- Creating flexibility to scale up or down the accounting services as needed.

ADVANTAGES THAT ACCRUE FROM OUTSOURCING

Lower employee costs. Outsourcing activities that only need to be done periodically saves on employee costs. A good example of this scenario is accounting services. Since accounting is a technical field, instead of hiring an accountant full time when the business is starting, services can be paid for only when required. The business also saves time and money associated with the recruiting, training, and onboarding of new staff.

More efficiency. Outsourcing leads to streamlined activities only being done in-house. As such, employees focus on tasks that they have expertise in and can do efficiently. Less time is wasted in learning to do things that are best outsourced. If particular care is taken to choose the best businesses to partner with, the outsourced work will be of exceptional quality that will make it easier for the business to achieve its value propositions.

Higher productivity. Less time is wasted on mundane tasks. Instead of tying down key employees on time-consuming work that can be done by anyone, outsourcing creates time that can be used on more productive work.

Reduced cost of doing business. Outsourcing key activities to a business that has a comparative advantage in that area will reduce the overall cost of production. To create maximum value for the business, the product development process must be scrutinized to identify all areas where cost savings can be made without compromising on quality. These cost savings can then be passed on to the customers as part of the business's value proposition.

Reduced risk of company failure. All new businesses have to take on a certain amount of risk, which, if not handled properly, can lead to failure early on in the business venture. By outsourcing some of the key activities to seasoned businesses, the new business is engaging in a form of risk management. For example, if outsourcing leads to lower overall production costs, the new business will, as a result, have a higher margin of safety. This implies that it can withstand business shocks better before going into the loss zone.

Economies of scale. Economies of scale can only be generated by businesses that have the resources and the customer base to support the large-scale production of products. By outsourcing to those businesses that can generate these economies, the new businesses can also get a slice of these economies, instead of trying to do everything in-house.

Time saved. Outsourcing to a business that has a lot of experience in the required field means that there is less likely to be unknowns that have to be figured out before a project can take off. This business, due to previous work done, understands the ecosystem well in that particular niche and has a lot of contacts and connections that can be called on to solve business-related issues in the most time-efficient manner. Trying to do everything yourself as a startup means having to deal with a lot of barriers to entry. In trying to solve issues, you may waste a lot of time.

Reduced errors. Outsourcing to experts means the business does not lose time and money trying to correct errors. A good example is accounting-related errors.

HOW TO CHOOSE THE RIGHT KEY PARTNERS

All the advantages listed above that can accrue from outsourcing can only be realized if the business has cracked the formula for finding the right key partners. The decision to outsource may be simply reached, but whom to partner with requires thorough research and a methodical approach based on objective information. The temptation that kills most businesses is to go with the business that charges the lowest prices to stretch the limited financial resources. However, this does not always lead to an optimal outcome. To choose the right partners, the following should be considered:

The Business's Goals

The business value proposition should go at the top of this list. In outsourcing, the business should not find itself compromising on the value proposition. Instead, effort should be made to find key partners who will make this value proposition a reality. Before looking for partners to partner with, the business should first work on understanding its own business goals and phrase these goals in a manner that will be understood by the partners that they choose to work with. When explaining these business goals, it is important to note that the other partners may not be as motivated as the internal team who came up with the value propositions. As such, before outsourcing, business goals need to be broken down into a list of specific requirements that are measurable, attainable, realistic, and time-bound. This will create a watertight contract that has no ambiguity.

For example, a business that has come up with an innovative plane idea may need to outsource the services of an engine manufacturer. Instead of just looking for a business partner that can manufacture a "strong engine," the list of requirements will have to be more specific. Specific thrust requirements, a certain level of efficiency and reliability, noise levels within certain decibels, and so on can be determined and laid out upfront as part of the design requirements. Outsourcing partners who can meet the design specifications can then be considered.

At the heart of outsourcing should be the value propositions. This essentially means checking if the outcome from the partnership will be a product that will appeal to the target market or not.

Industry Experience

A proven track record is a more objective criterion for choosing a business partner. Given a choice between competing partners, it is usually best to go with the one with more industry experience. Outsourcing to a newbie business may increase the risk of doing business. Check if the business being considered as a key partner understands the following;

- Industry best practices
- Nuances of the sector
- Rules and regulations

Access to key resources. If, as a business, you are outsourcing because you do not have access to the technology that you need to produce the product, then you should, before committing, inspect access to these technologies.

Project competence. Depending on what it is that is being outsourced, project competence can be seen through experienced staff, appropriate qualifications, process flow, and flexibility.

Communication. For a partnership to work, communication channels should be clear and predefined. Check for possible language barriers, especially when outsourcing to an overseas business partner, before committing to anything.

Time zone implications. Some time zone differences may make it impossible to have a viable business partnership. If your employees have to be up at midnight to attend to issues because of time zone issues, this arrangement may frustrate them, resulting in reduced productivity.

Ease with which work can be synchronized. Outsourced work should merge seamlessly with work that is produced in-house. This means that care should be taken when choosing a partner to ensure that this is possible, including looking at measurement standards and quality control methods. Failure to do this can cost the business tons of money and set it back from achieving its objectives, especially when there is negative publicity. Classic examples of the importance of this point are issues that arose between NASA and their outsourcing partner Lockheed Martin Astronautics in 1999. The contractors used imperial units when exchanging vital data, while the NASA spacecraft engineer team was expecting metric units. This failure to convert measurements cost NASA US $125 million.

ACTIVITIES THAT SHOULD NOT BE OUTSOURCED

While the advantages that a business can accrue are many, some activities are best kept within the company. As you consider the different ways to make your new business more efficient and cost-effective, keep in mind that letting go of some key activities may choke the business and lead to failure. Outsourcing should be approached cautiously and with a critical eye.

Core Business Competencies

If, as a business, you understand your sources of core competencies, then you should try to keep functions that are related to these in-house. A core competency is something that is at the heart of creating value for the business. Core competencies arise from the business possessing rare and difficult-to-replicate resources and capabilities. Instead of outsourcing, the business should exert effort in cultivating and exploiting its core competencies as a way of establishing itself in the market. Sometimes, competencies result from the execution of the business's mission. Relying on a third party to carry out core competencies means that the business is no longer in control and has abdicated responsibility for value creation to another company.

Functions That Depend on Proprietary Company Information

Intellectual capital should be kept in-house as much as possible. Some of these are embedded in human capital such as employee knowledge and unique skills developed over time, secret formulas and recipes, specific processes, and methods that result in the business having a competitive edge. Outsourcing any of these things means that the business then has to reveal its trade secrets. With this exposure, it becomes difficult to control these trade secrets and build upon these for the company to grow. Good examples of trade secrets are the Kentucky Fried Chicken (KFC) recipe, the Coca-Cola recipe, and the Google search algorithm. These companies guard these trade secrets jealously and go to great lengths to ensure that no other businesses get a hold of these. As such, it is best to avoid outsourcing if it means divulging trade secrets

Functions That May Result in Legal Penalties If Not Handled Properly

Outsourcing may leave the business at risk of legal liability. A contract entered into between the business and its customers does not necessarily extend to third parties that the business may choose to subcontract. In most cases, the business remains legally liable, while the third party may only have a contractual liability that stipulates that they reimburse the money paid. If things go wrong, however, the business has to bear the legal penalties, diversion of senior management's focus, and public embarrassment if the issue goes public. If the risk of legal liability is too much, it is best to do these functions in-house. An exception is made to work outsourced to licensed professionals. Such professionals are bound by the service provider's standard of care, ethical duties, and professional liability as defined under the statute and common law (Outsourcing Law Global, n.d.)

Functions in a Business That Are Volatile

It is best to outsource activities when you can define the exact nature of requirements and specifications for quality control purposes. There are, however, some business activities that may require decisions to be made on the fly and unorthodox solutions to problems that may arise. If that is the case, such business functions are best kept in-house, where there are key personnel who have internalized the business value propositions and are capable of making decisions that will further the value proposition drive.

Keeping such functions in-house also means that those tasked with the activities have at their disposal the support of in-house resources that can aid them in making the best decisions. Ad hoc meetings can be arranged, algorithms checked, and a decision made swiftly. If such a business function has been outsourced, it will not be possible for all decisions to go through this rigorous process. Outsourcing is best only when there is transparency in the production and delivery process and no ambiguity in the product specifications.

KEY PARTNERSHIPS

Forming strong partnerships with your ecosystem is an essential skill that can help expand your reach in any market and deliver value propositions to the target customers. Some examples of essential partnerships in business include:

- Alliances: These are entities that can work with you to make it possible to deliver your value propositions. Examples are joint ventures, relationships with a parent company, or partnership agreements.
- Suppliers: These are entities that provide inputs that you need to produce the product and the embedded value propositions.

Once you understand what activities will be outsourced and those that are best kept in-house, it is possible to fill in the key partners' block in the business model canvas. In this building block, you list the tasks and activities that are important but which you will not do yourself or do not have time for. Instead, you will use suppliers and partners to make the business model work. Continuous assessment and evaluation of the business's key partners should be part of the business strategy. It may be necessary to change key suppliers, for example, if the quality of their products is compromising the delivery of your value propositions.

For Google, the key partners' block would include the following:

Key partners for Google

- Internet users
- Websites in need of search engines
- Developers
- Content creators

CHAPTER 3: KEY ACTIVITIES

Key activities are defined as what your business is engaged in primarily to make a profit. This definition is not limited to activities that result in the production of the product but also encompass all activities necessary so that value is realized by the business. Production, operations, marketing, and administration activities that bring about the business's value proposition fall under key activities.

Any business, in its day-to-day operations, performs innumerable activities. All these activities, if listed in detail, cannot be concisely represented on the business model canvas without being truncated. Of all these activities, which ones are key?

To identify key activities that should go into the business model, one has to sift through all these activities and identify those that contribute toward differentiating the business's product from those of its competitors. Through this process, the sources of the business's competencies will be identified. A term that aptly defines this is a competitive advantage.

Competitive advantage refers to the attributes of a business that enables it to outperform its competitors. This set of attributes is, however, not static. A business operates in an ever-changing economic environment that is fraught with risk. Competitive advantage does not just come into being. It has to be created and maintained through continuously aligning the business to the business environment. At the inception of the business, it is paramount that the industry is scanned diligently to determine barriers to entry, level of product differentiation in the market, competitors, and the level of demand. These factors will then feed into a strategy formulation that will give a business the attributes needed to outperform its competitors.

Having a competitive advantage means that the business possesses attributes that enable it to produce a product more efficiently than its competitors. This competitive advantage results in the business offering more value to its customers. Some examples of how a business can create more value for customers are listed below:

A differentiated product: Differentiated products are a direct outcome of product innovation. Production innovation is the process through which a business implements new ideas that result in either a unique product or a more effective process or service. The launch of a differentiated product disrupts the market equilibrium. As the market adjusts, room is created for the new product, and other products that are perceived to be inferior are demoted. Product differentiation is the catalyst that fast tracks a business's journey to success. However, changing market forces require that innovation not be a once-off thing. Each business, startups included, should make innovation a part of the business culture and should stand ready, poised to explore promising leads that could lead to a differentiated product.

Using product differentiation, a business can position itself to produce a product that far outperforms that of competitors in the same segment in terms of durability, features, and benefits. If these features directly pander to the customers' needs, customers are likely to see this product as more superior to that of the competitors. This differentiation can enable the business to charge higher prices for the product and still get a lion's share of the market. In this case, the company will be competing on the market using quality.

Minimal costs in the production process: Coming up with lean and more efficient systems and processes can increase both efficiency and productivity. The most immediate advantage of this is the lower costs in the business. Lower production costs can spawn off advantages that can help the business grow in leaps and bounds through:

- Creating wider profit margins for the business that cannot be matched by competitors. With wider profit margins, the business can excel even in volatile markets. This ability to survive in adverse market conditions gives the business an edge over competitors who may close when hard times hit.
- Cost savings that can be passed on to the customers in the form of lower prices

without compromising the business's profit margins. This may be what makes the firm stand out from competitors and entices customers to try the firm's products. There are many market penetration strategies that a new business can try when launching a product. A popular strategy is to offer a new product at a price that is low enough to tantalize target consumers to choose the new product over competitor products.

- Sometimes, lower costs are exactly what it will take to meet customer needs. Some products are targeted at high-income groups because of high production costs. This does not necessarily mean that the demand for the product is not there among the low-income groups. A company that can come up with an innovative approach to produce this product at a lower cost is likely to capture the lion's share of the market, thus tapping into previously inaccessible revenue streams.

Any activities that contribute toward the realization of minimal production costs are key activities.

Human resources: If a business can hire the best people and then develop these people to be part of the business's competitive advantage, it has struck gold. The driving force behind the most successful business ventures is the people behind.

At the core of all successful businesses are uniquely talented individuals who work efficiently as part of a team to differentiate the business from competitors. It is people hired by the company who come up with innovative ideas and work tirelessly to bring these ideas to life. It is also people who create a unique corporate culture and work hard at making it become part of a recognizable brand. People also come up with ways to give customers a unique experience that will make them want to go back for more. It is no wonder why businesses spend a lot of time and resources on the hiring process. This is to ensure that only those people who fit in and can contribute positively to the business's vision are taken on board. Competitors may try to replicate your products, but they can never do this with your employees. As such, activities that are people-centric like brainstorming sessions and customer service can be a competitive advantage.

HOW TO WRITE THE KEY ACTIVITIES BUILDING BLOCK

Before writing the key activities building block, the prerequisites that should be written down in no ambiguous terms are:

- The business's value propositions
- The distribution channels that will be used
- The customer relationships that need to be developed
- The revenue streams

This block can only be written effectively if reference is made to the other blocks on the business model canvas. With reference to the prerequisites, the critical activities that need to be performed for the business to achieve and maintain a competitive advantage can be deduced. Key activities can be broken down into the following categories:

Production Key Activities

These are activities that are directly related to creating a product with a competitive advantage and getting it in front of the consumers. This could be design work, actual manufacturing processes, and thinking of unique ways that the product can be delivered to the customer in line with the business's value propositions. As such, typical key activities include design work, production, and marketing.

Problem-Solving Key Activities

Problem-solving is all about coming up with solutions to unique problems. A good example of this is customer service. Each customer presents a problem that is different from the next, and solutions have to be customized to suit the customer's circumstances. Businesses that have problem-solving as a huge part of their value proposition include service organizations such as realtors, lawyers, consultancies, and mortgage bankers. For problem-solving to be done effectively, there have to be two key activities built into the business model from inception: knowledge management and continuous training.

Knowledge management is the conscious process of defining, structuring, retaining, and sharing the knowledge and experience of employees within a business (Valamis, n.d.). This improves efficiency in the decision-making process, increases productivity, and can also create competitive advantages. For example, a business that is known for its exceptional customer service will most likely have invested a lot of time and effort in knowledge management and the creation of unparalleled resources such as:

- A well-written, easy-to-follow, and always up-to-date list of frequently asked questions.
- Clear processes to guide customer service assistants on how to quickly and efficiently access the information that is required by clients. Most customers appreciate and value highly the ability to resolve issues in a timely fashion.
- A team of experienced personnel who share their knowledge with recruits as part of inducting them into the company
- Frequent "know your product" training sessions for staff. Excellent customer service can only be offered by frontline staff who fully appreciate what the product's features, uses, and advantages are and know how to troubleshoot. For this to happen, different departments have to work together and share their knowledge with the frontline staff.
- A systematic method of collecting information about the different types of customers, their wants and needs, and their

honest feedback on how customer service can be improved. Infusing this information into the customer service model creates a more focused, customized, and personalized approach to customer service.

Platform/Network Key Activities

Most business models can only be executed successfully if supported by platform/network-related key activities. A good example is a banking institution. In addition to the physical branches where customers can go in person to get services, a bank provides more value to its customers by making available and managing several ATMs in various places that are easily accessible to their customers. The bank also needs to create various platforms such as online and cellphone banking to enable its customers to link to other service providers through the use of their credit cards for online purchases. Typical platform/network-related key activities for a bank will include ensuring system uptime through IT operations and ATM maintenance.

Some businesses are purely platform businesses. For example, job sites where most freelancers get work are platform businesses. The platform becomes a marketplace that brings together those who are looking for work as freelancers and those who need freelance workers. The platform provider creates value for themselves by controlling this platform and making it as efficient and seamless as possible. Key platform/network-related activities include platform management, service provision, and platform promotion.

The Recruitment Process

Most value propositions can only be delivered successfully if the business has employed the right people who fit in with the business corporate culture. The focus of the recruitment process in such a case is not just about talent and skill set. Cultural fit is a key factor, and it is only those on the inside who can best understand what kind of people are likely to fit in. The business's values, beliefs, decision-making process, communication process, and other such nuances live within the people who have been part of the business. It is people who have embraced the culture who should play a leading role in the recruitment process.

When looking at the key activities for Google, they would be:

> ## Key activities for Google
> - Developing the search algorithm
> - Data indexation
> - Research and development
> - Marketing and selling

FAILURE TO IDENTIFY KEY ACTIVITIES

Failure to identify key activities that can complement the business's value-adding propositions can lead to the following issues:

- Failure to secure and maintain a market share. Fighting to maintain the market share a business has is an ongoing activity. Each business should identify its key activities and continuously seek to consolidate these to avoid losing market share to competitors.
- Falling productivity and efficiency. Value can only be talked about in relation to customers. As technology evolves and new competing products are developed, the

business must ensure it keeps up with the industry pace. Processes that might have been deemed efficient a few years back may have been overtaken by new technologies, and a failure to adapt may mean that the business is relatively less productive and efficient.

- Losing key staff.
- Experiencing steadily reducing margins and profit.
- Going out of business.

When coming up with your business model, properly identifying key activities hinges on identifying and understanding the company's value propositions first. With this done, it will then be easier to align all key activities (operations) toward achieving the value propositions.

CHAPTER 4: KEY RESOURCES

Key resources in the business model canvas are "the set of difficult to trade and imitate, scarce, appropriate and specialized resources and capabilities that bestow the firm's competitive advantage" (Olokundun, 2014). These resources are necessary for the business to do the following:

- Deliver value propositions embedded in the product
- Create and maintain distribution channels
- Create and maintain customer relationships
- Realize revenue streams

A critical review of what the business intends to achieve will make it possible to answer the following questions:

1. Is the business capital intensive?
2. How best can these resources be acquired? Is it better to lease these resources, own them, or find a business partner with access to these resources?
3. What kind of human resources does the business need to create and deliver its value propositions?

Not all businesses are created equal. Each business may have unique capital requirements, leading to variations in the definition of what key resources are. As such, it is important to analyze the business and identify the different types of resources that the business already has, those that it can leverage, and those that need to be outsourced. Core competencies are distinctive, rare, valuable firm-level resources that competitors are unable to imitate, substitute, or reproduce.

WHY IS IT IMPORTANT TO KNOW YOUR KEY RESOURCES?

Most businesses start based on an idea of a product with distinct value propositions. With these value propositions in mind, an effort to identify key resources will help you focus on the internal environment as a driver for competitive advantage. Questions that you will need to answer when coming up with a business plan are:

- What resources do you need to make it possible to deliver this product?
- What resources do you already have that will give you a competitive edge in the delivery of these value propositions?
- How best can these key resources be acquired?
- Is it possible to develop the capabilities of some of these resources and make them unable to be replicated?
- What is the best way to deploy these key resources?

For most new businesses, it is easier for the business to try and change its internal environment and develop competitive advantages than to focus on trying to beat competition without the capabilities to do so. Consider a business that tries to differentiate its product based on price. Its value proposition of "lowest price in the industry" will be a failure if its internal environment is not geared to create this value proposition. To deliver this value proposition, the business will have to lower its prices should other businesses come in with cheaper prices. A different approach leading to the same value proposition would be to take an inside-out view.

If the company owns strategic assets that enable it to mass-produce products of a competitive quality but at a lower price, then this value proposition is sustainable. There is a clear competitive advantage that is brought about just from having these assets and knowing how to deploy them. From this perspective, the business is likely to succeed, even if competitors try to undercut prices.

WHY BOTHER IDENTIFYING KEY RESOURCES?

Key resources help the business refine its value propositions. Some value propositions are brought about by assets that the business has. An analysis of how best to use these assets can help you realize these value propositions. At the same time, the realization of some value propositions hinges on access to key resources. Some good product ideas do not make it to the market due to a lack of key resources necessary to produce the product at a reasonable cost. An analysis of key resources needed should be part of the feasibility test when coming up with business ideas.

Additionally, key resources are important because:

- They are an integral part of the business's core competencies.
- You can enter into strategic partnerships to gain access to resources that can put you in a better position to deliver your value proposition.
- Approximations of capital requirements will be more detailed once the key resources needed have been identified. Most startup businesses start with great ideas that have good market potential. The underestimation of key resources needed then leads to inadequate financial resources sourced. As a result, efforts to cut costs may lead the business to cut corners to make ends meet.

This then compromises the quality of the product, resulting in a mismatch between the value proposition and the product that is delivered to the market.

- Acknowledgment of key resources gives the business idea value and credibility. When a business idea is being pitched to various stakeholders, pointing out the key resources needed and how these can be accessed makes the idea more tangible. As a result, a business that has done its homework well in filling in the key resources block is likely to get more buy-in.

- Acknowledging key resources can give rise to a more focused and sustainable business strategy, one that shows how to best use the available resources to create value for the business.

THE FOUR IMPORTANT CATEGORIES OF KEY RESOURCES

Resources can be broadly classified into four categories: physical, intellectual, human, and financial. When filling in the business model canvas, only those assets that are strategically important should be listed. These are assets and competencies that give the business a competitive edge. Ideally, these assets should be distinctive and not easily replicated by competitors. Without these key resources, it may not be easy to deliver the key value propositions.

Physical Assets as a Key Resource

These are assets that are material in nature and typically capital intensive. Examples of these are buildings, vehicles, machines, tools, and distribution networks. They are the most visible form of how valuable a business is as they are enumerated on a business's financial statements. Access to these physical resources helps the business unlock other key resources that are necessary to create a competitive edge. A good example is a business that needs a long-term bank loan to fund an innovative product idea. A business that owns a building that can be used as collateral is likely to get a loan with more favorable terms than one that does not have any significant assets on its balance sheet.

The worth of physical assets as a form of competitive edge in delivering the business value proposition is seen through the business strategy. This strategy will reveal how these assets can be paired with technology and deployed to increase production capacity and productivity and boost business operations.

How to Identify Key Physical Resources for the Business Model Canvas

Assets that give you a competitive edge are the only ones that should go on the business model canvas. After identifying all your physical needs, the next step is to critically analyze how each one helps you deliver a unique value proposition. For example, let's assume you are considering venturing into a business and you have just signed a lease agreement on a property. A good starting place to determine if this is a key resource is to ask what it is about that property that is going to contribute to your success.

If the business idea is purely online-based, then this lease is not necessarily a key resource. Many successful virtual companies do not have a physical office space! Good examples of these are FlexJobs, Hubstaff, GitLab, and Sutherland Global Services (Stillman, 2016). If you are considering going into retail, however, factors that can make this resource key are location and the physical attributes of the property as discussed below:

Location: The location of a property makes it easier to reach the target customers. When justifying how location gives you a competitive edge, factors that should be looked at include the following:

1. Catchment size, which is the sphere of influence area around the store that makes it easier for the business to draw in target customers. The socio-demographics of people who live within the catchment area affect the potential level of demand, the traffic that you might get in the store, and the relevance of your product.
2. Stakeholder impression. New business ideas face a lot of resistance, and part of managing that resistance is to create a good first impression. A business address can determine the ease with which customers are persuaded to try out a new retail outlet.
3. Accessibility. How well the business will take off also depends on how easily accessible it is to both customers and employees. A location where there are no good transport links may mean that the business has to shoulder the burden to provide transport for its

employees, which may increase operating costs.

4. Rents and rates. The location heavily determines the rents and rates and, by extension, the profit margins that are likely to be earned.

Physical attributes: Physical attributes determine the ease with which the store can be customized to provide the best customer service and differentiate itself from the competition. A store that has access to a private parking lot, for example, is likely to help provide a pleasant customer experience and guarantee a hustle-free entry and exit. Failure to find a safe parking space close enough to a store to make shopping convenient is usually a source of frustration for most customers. The business can piggyback on this physical attribute to provide more value for its customers by providing parking lot security, which will reduce risk concerns for customers. It may also mean customers can spend a lot more time in the store without worrying about parking charges. If the business is innovative, it can provide smart parking management infrastructure as a way of differentiating itself from competitors through the use of smart technology. If at the entrance to the parking lot, a customer is directed to the best open spot instead of wasting time circling and looking for an open space, customers are likely to be delighted with the service.

A purely online retail store, however, when considering how key a property is, will look at different factors. Since customers are online, catchment size and all the other factors discussed above may not matter. Key physical resources may be delivery trucks and access to large warehouses from which distribution routes can be mapped easily.

Key Intellectual Resources

These assets are a subset of intangible assets. Intellectual resources are valuable to the firm and unique in the sense that they are the result of past events, and yet the business can strategically use them to achieve future economic benefits. Examples of these intellectual assets are patents, licenses, customer databases, brand names, specialist knowledge, trademarks and copyrights, partnerships, customer databases, franchise agreements, domain names, and trade secrets.

These resources are generally diverse. It is not possible to find two businesses having the same brand name or domain names. This diversity makes them a valuable source of competitive advantage as they are resistant to duplication. Intellectual resources are also immobile. They cannot be easily transferred to other businesses, which gives the business a valuable resource—time to come up with a strategy to maximize value from the use of these resources.

Human Resources as a Key Resource

People are a resource since they are the ones who transform resources into value propositions. This is particularly true in creative and knowledge-intensive industries where the secret behind the success of a business is to hire the right people. This is why a lot of businesses are willing to spend a lot of money on the recruitment process. Competitors can never duplicate the people you hire, which essentially makes each business unique. Intellectual property such as designs and trademarks help a business establish its presence on the market. People who have proprietary know-how are instrumental in creating key sources of competitive advantage that, if exploited, can yield income for years.

In the service industry, a key resource is the human resource that is owned by a business. Service quality is largely dependent on the ability to serve and how motivated and creative the staff is. This human side of the company affects the speed and flexibility of the service offered. People are also the face of the company and are essentially the business's brand. People are an essential part of most business strategies, and a lot of effort is channeled toward developing this key resource.

Depending on the type of business, the following could be listed as key human resources in the business model canvas:

Work experience of key personnel: For example, to open a retail pharmacy business, state regulations list one of the requirements to get a license as having access to a full-time, registered, practicing pharmacist who will supervise the business.

Abilities of staff: For a web design business, key personnel would be people who are skilled in graphics designing, front-end development technologies, and content management.

Notable achievements: For a consulting business, success hinges on the ability of the business to attract clients. The business will first have to convince its customers that the personnel in the business are experts in a particular field and are better suited to provide unique and differentiated quality service that will be more beneficial to the customer. Certifications, special licensing, and awards can attract the clientele needed to make the business a success.

Key Financial Resources

Examples of financial resources are lines of credit and cash balances. These resources determine if innovative strategies that the firm comes up with can be brought to life or not. A lack of financial resources is the most common resource behind the curtailing of innovative and potentially profitable strategies. Physical resources on their own are not enough to aid a business in delivering a value proposition. Financial resources help provide money for the following:

- Day-to-day operating costs. These costs need to be covered even when the business hasn't started realizing any revenue streams. For example, at the end of each month, staff salaries, rent, and other day-to-day expenses need to be paid.
- Research and development costs.

- Marketing-related research costs.
- Expansion purposes. A business may need to buy assets to create and/or maintain its competitive edge. If required assets are capital intensive, only those businesses with access to financial resources can create and benefit from the competitive advantage this will yield.

For most startups, there are usually negative cash flows in the early months. This is because startup costs have to be paid upfront. As a result, a lack of adequate finances can easily become a barrier to entry even when one has a good business idea.

The key activities for Google will include the following:

Key resources
- Google's secret algorithm
- Googlebot- the program that scans the net
- Staff talent
- Google's many platforms that are used to deliver their value propositions
- Patents
- Infrastructure (search engines require huge amounts of computing resources)

PATHWAYS TO DETERMINING KEY RESOURCES

Three methods can be used together to come up with a comprehensive list of key resources.

1. **Start with key resources to determine value propositions.** Using this method, you determine what key resources you have and then come up with product ideas modeled around these key resources.

2. **Start with the value propositions to determine key resources**. This method works well if you already have a good product idea and value propositions that will make the product sell. You can then use these product ideas and work backward to determine the key resources needed to deliver these value propositions.

3. **Start with industry analysis**. Start with a product idea, and then scope out the key resources owned by the most successful companies. You will then have to figure out how to differentiate your product and the key resources needed to achieve that.

Coming up with key activities should not be a one-time event but should, instead, be an iterative process as you refine the business model canvas. As such, the use of any of these three methods will yield value. Each method forces you to look at the business model from a different perspective. To be thorough, you can use all three methods to ensure that you have covered all bases. Keep in mind that competitive advantages are usually short-lived. Changes in technology and the business environment can diminish competitive advantages. As such, it is vital to keep abreast of news, evaluate changes in the industry, and react in a manner that helps consolidate and maintain the business's competitive advantages. For example, if new technology makes it possible for other businesses to produce a product at a cheaper cost, a feat that could only be achieved by a few companies like yours, it might be worth it as a business to explore if acquiring that same technology can help you defend your niche market.

Value propositions are the reasons that convince customers to choose your business over competitors. These value propositions can be embedded in the product itself or in the processes and methods used in the creation of the product, or they can result from how you conduct business. Through this value proposition, benefits that accrue to customers from conducting business with you should be crystal clear. The value propositions should form the foundation of any marketing campaign and should lure customers who are likely to benefit the most. A value proposition can be any of the following or a combination thereof:

- A company's promise to its customers about

the value they are likely to get from choosing the product.

- A statement that describes what the company's values are and how these are incorporated in the way the company conducts business.
- Why the company deserves the support of its target customers.

After careful thought, it should be possible to come up with a simple and clear statement that succinctly summarizes all these points from the customer's perspective. Thus, value proposition statements will be the foundation on which a lot of marketing promotions will be built, including brand strategy, taglines, and customer outreach programs. A good value proposition can only be crafted if the business understands its competitive advantage.

WHY IS COMPETITIVE ADVANTAGE IMPORTANT FOR A STARTUP?

Attributes that set your business apart from competitors will make your presence felt. Your target group is likely to notice if your product appears to address an existing problem in a unique way. In this global business world, competition is stiff. At the same time, globalization has opened up worldwide markets that enable even a small competitive advantage to yield significant cash flows due to borderless markets. The key to getting competitive advantages is brand recognition. If your product's brand is associated with a tangible competitive advantage, the initial investment made in developing this brand will pay off. Value propositions should, as such, be geared toward highlighting superiority over competitors. Examples are:

- Quality products at a lower cost
- Great customer care or the best support, which equals more value for money
- Premium quality products that last longer

HOW TO COME UP WITH A VALUE PROPOSITION

A successful business is one that can create and realize value from its product offering. That said, it is not enough to just come up with a great product. Effort should be invested in demonstrating how valuable this product is to the target customers by highlighting the needs and problems that the product solves.

To create a value proposition, the business has to first invest a lot of time and research into understanding the customers' wants and needs and how existing products are falling short of meeting these needs. This analysis will demonstrate the gap in the market. The business should then show how this particular product uniquely satisfies these wants and needs. The value proposition serves to connect the product that the company has with the customer base that makes it possible for the business to realize value. After all, a business without customers is as good as a body that is starved of oxygen. The collapse of the business will only be a matter of time.

A lot of effort has to be invested into coming up with a simple and clear value proposition statement that succinctly summarizes the knowledge about the product on one hand and the knowledge about the customers' wants and needs on the other. The value proposition statement should bring to the fore the following three things:

- **Relevance.** You have a new product on the market, but so what? How does this product solve customers' needs? Does it improve the customer's situation in any way?

- **Quantified value.** Are there any specific benefits that the customer is likely to get from the product?
- **Differentiation.** What makes your product different from other competitive businesses that have similar products?

BENEFITS OF A GOOD VALUE PROPOSITION

If a value proposition is done right, benefits that will accrue to the company include:

- Helping position the product competitively. To position a product is to create an identity of the product in the customers' minds. If, whenever customers see your product, the first thing that pops into their minds is one of the value propositions, then the product has been positioned competitively.
- Engaging copy material that will draw in target customers to read more about the product, thus increasing product awareness.
- Persuasive power over customers.

TYPES OF VALUE PROPOSITIONS

Depending on what type of product you have to offer, you can draw on the following example elements for inspiration when coming up with a value proposition:

Newness. Newness can be looked at from two distinct perspectives: new to the company and new to the customers. From a company's perspective, new may mean any of the following:

- **Product replacements:** This is when a company takes one of its existing products and repositions it or makes adjustments to the production process to reduce production costs.
- **Addition to existing product lines:** A good example is the decision to offer an existing product in different sizes and/forms. If previously, the company was selling 1-pound soap bars, and they decided to also package the same soap as 8-ounce soap bars, this is a new product. The company can also decide to offer the same soap in liquid form.
- **New product line:** This is the addition of a new product that did not previously exist in

the company's portfolio. For example, when a company that was concentrating on manufacturing children's toys decides to move into children's clothes, then a new product line is created.

A common oversight that most businesses make when coming up with value propositions is to use this company perspective and stop there. The target customer is not necessarily tied to the company and has access to a wide array of products from different businesses to choose from. This highlights the importance of donning the customer's shoes and looking at the value proposition as a customer. From the customer's perspective, newness can be subdivided using the following classification:

- **Continuous innovation:** This kind of newness has minimal impact on the behavioral patterns of consumers. The new product will essentially be an existing product that has undergone marginal changes designed to improve the product and give the customers more benefits. Care should be taken when coming up with the value proposition for such a product as customers may not notice the difference between the new product and the existing product despite a lot of money having been invested in the business idea. A carefully crafted value proposition statement will point out these differences and heighten the customers' perceptions.

- **Dynamically continuous innovation:** This kind of newness relates to existing products as well but requires moderate adaptation to existing behavioral patterns if the product is to be successful.

- **Discontinuous innovation:** This kind of innovation challenges some of the essential perceptions and habits of the customers. Success hinges on creating new behavioral patterns on the part of the consumer. While product differentiation may be clearly visible with this kind of innovation, the biggest hurdle may be to deal with resistance to change and getting the target customer to be an innovator. This discontinuous innovation from a company's perspective is a "new to the world" product.

The company has to come up with a unique product requiring a new market altogether. A new product like this implies that it's the first of its kind and consumers have nothing to compare it with. The biggest risk with this kind of product is the high failure rate due to non-acceptance by the market. This risk of product failure highlights the importance of a value proposition. Creating a new market requires that the firm equips itself with new marketing skills to serve this entirely new-to-the-firm customer base that might have different wants and needs from those that the business normally deals with. A challenge that also has to be faced is the lack of historical information about this kind of customer. The company has to engage in a lot of research and use this to leverage product advantages that arise from newness.

Design. Design is not only limited to making a product beautiful. It is a concept that should be integrated into all processes that ultimately lead to value creation, including research and development, communications, and marketing. Design helps the business's value proposition stand out and, as a result, makes it possible for the business to position its product offering competitively. Through design, the company's brand also becomes more recognizable to customers, which helps boost sales. Design as a value proposition can take several forms, discussed below.

When a product is looked at from a customer's perspective and then designed with the customer in mind, the outcome is usually a simplified, less complex, efficient, easy-to-use, and cost-effective product. A product like this is likely to be more attractive to customers and seen as more value for money.

For data-rich products, great product design that would act as a value proposition would take into account information architecture and user experience. A good example of a data-rich product is the use of telemetry in the car insurance industry.

Insurance companies are looking for different ways to differentiate their products. More and more insurance companies are seeking to customize premiums charged by using the information on the driving habits of the client, which has resulted in new insurance products such as pay-as-you-drive and usage-based insurance. An insurance company seeking a good telemetry product to buy that can provide the data needed for this purpose would not just purchase any product that is available on the market. Special attention would be paid to how the product is designed by looking at both information architecture and user experience. This platform is data-rich in the sense that it will be collecting a lot of data for each client by tracking the movement of each car. However, it is not just information about where a particular client's car was at a particular time that will yield useful information for the insurance company. How this collected data is packaged will determine the ease with which useful information can be inferred from the collected information, including:

- How many miles their clients drive a year
- The time of day and locations that a vehicle is driven
- The drivers' braking, acceleration, speeding, turning, and cornering behaviors

If the product is well-designed, correlations and insights and other statistics can be drawn from the information that will point to the level of aggressiveness of the driver, proficiency in controlling a vehicle, and the probability of the car being driven during crash peak periods. All this information combined yields a more accurate risk assessment profile that can then be used for differentiated pricing. In designing such a product, information architecture should take into account the user's end goal and needs. The customer user experience should also be optimized by simplifying workflow, which is the steps that one needs to take to accomplish a goal. Great product design can ensure that the customer user experience is great and will result in the product ranking high among competitors.

Brand/Status. This value proposition positions the product as a more superior product compared to what is available on the market. The success of this value proposition hinges on understanding what customers value in a product and then pointing this out. If the product is easily replicable, this value proposition can only yield benefits to the business for a short while, unless it is combined with other not-so-easy-to-replicate attributes. Design highly complements this value proposition and helps position the product. A good example is how a good design helps highlight the value of the Apple MacBook when compared to other personal computers. Innovative design enables the Apple brand to sell for more than six times the cost of other personal computers.

Price. Price-sensitive customers respond very well to a value proposition that offers the same level of functionality as competing brands for a lower price. However, for this proposition to pan out and create value for both the customers and the business, the manufacturing and distribution process should be stripped and made lean. The goal will be to create efficient processes to make cost savings that will be passed on to the consumer. If your prices are the lowest on the market, the value proposition is clear and is something that customers can resonate with and get tangible benefits from. However, defending this value proposition may be difficult. Any company can decide to undercut your businesses and sell at a lower price and make losses in a bid to squeeze you out of business.

In addition, price is used to complement other value propositions chosen by a business. For example, the value that a product has cannot, in the customers' mind, be separated from the price that is charged. Where the customers' value proposition is premium branding, customers will also expect relatively higher prices to be charged. If the company's value proposition is cost leadership, then this should be visible to the customer in lower product prices for the same functionality.

Risk reduction. Insurance is a good example of a product whose main value proposition is risk mitigation. Insurance clients are willing to pay money to transfer the financial implications of events that may or may not occur in the future. In general business, your customers are also confronted by risks that include the following:

- Misunderstanding the value proposition of the product
- Product obsolescence
- Lack of post-sale support

These risks may make the customer hesitate to commit to buying a product. Understanding these risks and designing risk mitigators that are not offered by your competitors not only helps demonstrate empathy with your target customers but can also help differentiate your product and create a value proposition that will resonate with customers who need these risk mitigators. Typical risk-reduction innovations that can be used as value propositions include the following:

- Free trials
- Money-back guarantees

- Risk-free guarantees
- 100% satisfaction guarantees
- Lifetime warranties
- Service-level agreements
- Low-price guarantee or price matching

Convenience. Convenience as a value proposition hinges on the ability of the business to eliminate customer friction. There may be a lot of equally good competing products on the market, but the ease with which customers can move through the marketing and sales funnel to access the product is different. Many customers end up buying a competing product not because it was their first choice, but because they got frustrated or annoyed in the process of trying to get their product of choice. Friction emanates from flaws in the product design and purchase and delivery processes. Convenience as a value proposition arises if a product is designed to address these flaws. If, as a business, you come up with a product that makes it more convenient and easier to achieve something, and this innovation improves customer experience, then you've got the makings of a winning value proposition.

To come up with convenience as a value proposition, the key is to compare the business's product with the point of differentiating it from competing products using known friction points. Ask yourself:

- Is your product more practical and easier to use? An example would be a more intuitive product interface.
- Is your product a solution that is more accessible to the majority of target customers than competing products?
- Is the product more functional? In other words, does it do what it is expected to do better than other products?
- What is the user experience like? Does your product enable the target market to access things in a more streamlined and more efficient faction? This, when compared to a website where the customer has to fumble to locate even the most basic functionalities to enable them to purchase the product, will attract customers.
- Are there any known errors or common issues in competing products that are notably not there in yours?
- Do competing products have a long and winding process that customers have to go through before they can access the product?

HOW TO WRITE A VALUE PROPOSITION

Before your business model can take off, you will have to get buy-in from a number of stakeholders, including financiers and customers. Financiers should be able to believe that the target customers will see value in your product. When preparing to write the value proposition, put yourself in the customer's shoes, and be clear.

Put yourself in the customer's shoes. Aim to come up with something that the customers can read, understand, and resonate with. The ideal value proposition statement should be simple and not riddled with technical jargon. It is not an easy decision for a customer to try your product. Instead of going with their proven go-to product that they have been using all along, they are debating whether or not they should choose yours. In most cases, resistance to change wins. A well-written value proposition can, however, tilt the scales in your favor and add an objective reason for the customer to try your product.

That said, for the value proposition to work, it has to be written from the customers' perspective. If the customers are to relate with the value proposition, the language used should be what the customer would use as well when describing the product's relevance, value, and differentiation.

Be clear. A good value proposition shouldn't leave the reader confused or unsure about what the statement means. As a rule of thumb, a good value proposition should be read and understood in about five minutes (Laja, 2019).

To round up this chapter, the picture below shows Google's value propositions.

Value propositions

- A superior search engine which returns more relevant search results than competitors
- Free email
- Instant messaging and chat
- Language translations
- Cloud computing services
- Google shopping which allows users to compare online prices across different vendors
- Mapping services

Segmenting is to break a market into subgroups of customers that have similar characteristics and, as a result, may have the same product needs. When a new product is thought of, the typical scenario in most businesses is that it is acknowledged that different customer segments may be interested in it. The product and the value propositions embedded in the product are designed to appeal to these 'known' groups of customers. This section of the business model canvas highlights the importance of knowing who these customers are and how to identify them.

A product that is designed from the start with this information in mind is likely to be designed and packaged in a way that appeals to these customer segments. This increases the chance of the product performing well on the market.

WHY ARE CUSTOMER SEGMENTS IMPORTANT?

Customers are an important foundation for the survival of any business. A business without customers does not have any revenue streams and will definitely fold. In trying to capture a slice of this critical resource, a business is better off focusing on segments for the following reasons:

Helps Refine Value Propositions

A one-size-fits-all approach is not the most efficient way to come up with a product that sells well. Each company, due to resource constraints, cannot effectively serve all customers in a market. Instead, when resources and competitive advantages are focused to serve particular segments, a better brand strategy is created. When market research is conducted on different segments, one of the key outcomes is the key motivators behind the demand for the product. This knowledge can then be used to further refine the product's value proposition to suit the target customers. The result from this process is a better-positioned product and a competitive edge over other companies serving the same market.

Helps Discover New Market Opportunities

As part of its overall strategy, a business should always be on the lookout for new business opportunities where it can have a competitive advantage. The process of breaking a market for a particular product into clusters can reveal niche markets that are not served by competitors. Understanding this niche's requirement and tailoring the product value propositions to suit this unserved market can give the business first-mover advantages. Just by being the first in the market, a business can lock in the following:

Strong brand recognition. A product that is introduced first will be tried and tested by many before new products are introduced. This product is likely to be widely recognized and preferred to newer products that enter the market as they will be perceived as 'wannabe' products

Customer loyalty. By the time other competitors enter the arena, they will have to battle resistance to change and other market barriers. Chief among these barriers is stiff competition from the business that entered the market first and is defending its market share.

Time to refine the product. As part of defending competitive advantages, businesses spend resources gathering feedback on customer satisfaction. This information is used to refine the product, strengthen customer relations, and create more competitive advantages. Being a first-mover buys the company time to create intellectual and human resources that are difficult to replicate and compete with. Examples of businesses with first-mover advantages in their respective niches are Coca-Cola, eBay, and Amazon.

Economies of scale. A longer time in the market combined with expertise and experience enables a business to develop more cost-efficient production processes. This combined with a lion's share of the market are essential factors for economies of scale. Consolidating the business in this manner creates barriers to entry and magnifies the business's competitive advantages, which sets the business up for success.

Creates Marketing Efficiency

Most startups are resource-constrained and, as such, do not have lots of financial resources to splash on blind marketing campaigns that everyone can see. That being so, marketing is an important part of the journey to success for new businesses. When the market is segmented, all this marketing communication is channeled straight to the target market that is likely to buy the product. This saves costs as more relevant channels are used to get to the customer. It also creates more relevant channels to reach customers that can contribute to the development of intellectual resources. Marketing efficiency refers to both the effectiveness of the marketing campaigns and the realization of goals from the marketing efforts at the lowest cost possible. Despite being resource-constrained, marketing is important for a startup because:

1. **It's how you introduce the business to the customers.** If your business is new to the block, no one knows that it exists, what products and value propositions you offer, and, of course, where the products can be bought. As such, product awareness is the first step toward building a customer base. Targeted marketing after segmenting a market leaves nothing to chance—the message is sent exactly where target

customers are most likely to see it, resulting in more marketing efficiency.

2. **It helps increase sales.** Marketing is the main medium of communication that can be used to reach the target customer. After customer awareness has been established, efforts to encourage the target customers to adopt the product, such as discounts, free product samples, and free trial periods, are communicated through marketing mediums. If the market has been segmented, these promotions can be customized to appeal to the customers who are most likely to buy the product. This information can also be used to refine distribution strategies.

3. **It saves time.** Time is a resource that should be used wisely in an environment fraught with competition. When the business launches a product with unique value propositions, competitors notice and strategize to maintain their market share. As such, continuous product innovation is happening in the market. The business has a short period that it can use to establish itself and create relations with customers before competitors come in with similar

substitutes. Segmentation helps promote the product faster.

TYPES OF CUSTOMER SEGMENTS IN THE BUSINESS MODEL CANVAS

Before you attempt to fill in this block on the business model canvas, you need to understand the different types of customer segments that exist. Using this information, you can then formulate a business strategy based on which customer segment you can best serve to create more value for the business. Blocks on the business model canvas should then be tailored to be in line with this business strategy. Value propositions, distribution channels, and effort put in managing customer relationships should be relevant and tailored to suit the customer segment that the business has consciously chosen to serve. There are five broad customer segments—mass markets, niche markets, diversified markets, multi-sided platform markets, and segmented markets (Strategyzer, 2019). The following sections look at each of these in turn and demonstrate how to tailor value propositions, distribution channels, and customer relations in the business model canvas.

Mass Markets

This approach views the market as a large, undifferentiated block. Customer backgrounds vary widely, which leads to the conclusion that the product is needed by almost every member of the society. Examples of mass-market products are paper towels, soap, gas, utilities, and other consumer staples. Examples of mass-market businesses are Amazon, Target, and Best Buy. These stores position themselves to appeal to a wide variety of customers from different walks of life.

Value proposition: Since the market is undifferentiated, the business creates value through economies of scale. Competitive advantages that make this value proposition possible arise mainly from cost efficiencies, which are then passed on to consumers. The business strategy circles around providing the lowest cost product through minimizing costs and profit margins. Profitability then arises from selling these products on a large scale.

Distribution channels: A distribution channel is the chain of businesses that a product passes through until it reaches the buyer. The best distribution channel is one that shortens this chain, like the direct-to-consumer model. For mass markets, the product is ideally sold by a producer directly to the end customer. This cuts out wholesalers and retailers, allowing customers to buy these goods at a relatively lower price than would have been the case if a longer distribution channel was used. Amazon as a producer sells directly to the end customer.

Customer relations: To reach these broad customer groups, mass marketing methods are used. Typically, platforms that can reach millions of viewers in a single showing are used. This inevitably leaves out pockets of customers with unique needs unserved. This broad approach does not focus on or cultivate relationships with customers with individual needs.

Niche Markets

A niche market is a small subset of a market that has its own unique needs and preferences that are different from the market at large. As a business strategy when entering a new market, the odds of success go up when the focus is on a niche market that has little or no competition. For example, it might be difficult to look for ways to differentiate your value proposition in a market for women's shoes where there are already a lot of competing businesses. However, the vegan fashion market is still growing and presents a potentially profitable market with lots of opportunities for new entrants. Focusing on this small segment and providing shoes that meet the specific set of customers is a niche market strategy.

Niche market value propositions: These have to be tailored to appeal to the unique needs of the identified niche. For this to work, you have to know the target customers who fall into this niche very well, including those things that motivate them to buy. This might entail conducting market research on customer segments and competitors. Information from this research can then be used in the development of a value proposition that not only directly appeals to the needs of the target group but is also differentiated from that of competitors in the niche. Since this market is typically small and has unique needs, products are unlikely to be produced on a scale that justifies the use of the traditional long distribution chain of producer, wholesaler, retailers, and distributors.

Diversified Markets

Diversification occurs when a company comes up with different products that have different value propositions targeted at two or more different niche markets. Each niche market will have to be assessed as described above. The value propositions for each product will need to be tailored to the needs of the customers in that niche. Each niche should also be supported by an appropriate business strategy. A business with diversified markets will have different and unrelated customer segments.

Multi-Sided Platform Markets

This is a product that creates value by bringing together groups of people with different needs. This is made possible by creating a platform that works as a marketplace to attract these different groups. The main value proposition for this product is the:

- Reduction of transaction costs
- Reduction of economic friction
- Coordination of services to make it worthwhile for all groups

The distribution channels that should be used should aim to get enough agents on each side. Uber is a good example of a multi-sided platform. Customer segmentation looks at both customers and drivers as follows:

Segmentation basis	Driver segmentation	Customer segmentation
Demographic	Age, socio-economic group, nationality	
Geographic	City, suburb	Home, work, typical locations
Usage patterns		Regular, infrequent
Offering	UberX, UberPOOL, UberBLACK	UberX, UberPOOL, UberBLACK

Source: Uenlue (2018)

Segmented Markets

Factors that can be used to segment a market include geography, demographic factors such as gender and age groups, and psychographic factors such as social status and lifestyle. The product offering in each case has to be fine-tuned to suit the needs of each segment. An ideal segment that is worth pursuing meets the following conditions (Lumen Learning, n.d.):

- **It is big enough to be measured.** A business strategy can only be crafted for a segment that is big enough for data to be collected. This data will then be used to determine if it's worth it to serve the segment
- **It is profitable.** A viable segment is one that has enough resources to purchase the

product. The level of demand should also be above the break-even point for the business. If demand is too low, the costs incurred to produce the product may be more than the revenue collected, resulting in a loss. Profitability is also determined by how cost-effective it is to reach this segment.

- **The segment should be stable.** If it's transient, by the time you get to execute your business idea, the segments will have vanished. A good example is the business opportunities that arose when COVID-19 cases started spiking. There was a run on hand sanitizers in shops, and as a result, a market was made up of people who needed access to homemade hand sanitizers. A lot of books and blog posts were written and video tutorials were made to address this. By the time some of these products hit the market, hand sanitizers were readily available in shops again.

- **The segment should be internally homogenous and externally heterogeneous.** This means that within the segment, potential customers should exhibit the same needs and preferences. When compared to other segments, these needs and preferences should be different. This will allow the business to clearly differentiate its product offering.

The customer segments for Google are shown below:

Customer segments

- Users
- Advertisers
- Web publishers
- Developers
- Content producers

CHAPTER 7: CHANNELS

Channels are the different ways that customers can access your products. Each channel comprises various institutions that facilitate the transactions necessary for the customer to buy the product and the physical exchange of the product. These channels determine if the business manages to attain its main objective—to create value for the business by creating value for the customers. In any business, there is a gap between the producer of a product and the customers who need this product. A channel works as a bridge that connects the two.

CRITICAL FUNCTIONS OF A CHANNEL

To bridge the gap between the business and its customers, a channel should perform three critical functions (The Monash University, n.d.)

1. **Transactional functions:** These are activities associated with buying and reselling a product and the risks associated with keeping a product in stock. Each intermediary involved in the channel has a role to play that ultimately leads to the payment for the product reaching the business.

2. **Logistical functions:** Logistical functions include assembling products, sorting them into appropriate categories, and transportation.

3. **Facilitating functions:** This is assistance rendered to members of a marketing channel and the end-user. The facilitating channel institution does not take people to the goods but facilitates the delivery of the product and, in some situations, provides post-purchase service and maintenance. Examples of institutions that help provide

these functions are banks, transport companies, and insurance companies. These institutions provide specialized services that support and add to the value of the product.

Having a good product with the most compelling value propositions does not mean that value has been created for the company. It takes the right channels to ensure that this product is converted into revenue, or else the business may fold due to liquidity shortages. To maximize business value, the product has to reach the end-user in the most efficient and cost-effective manner. Choosing the best channel for your product is critical to business success.

TYPES OF DISTRIBUTION CHANNELS

Distribution channels can be broadly classified into four types—direct selling, selling through intermediaries, dual distribution, and reverse channels (recycling products or product recalls). Below, we will look at the first three, which take the product from the business to the customer.

Direct Selling

This is when as a producer of a product, you sell straight to the customer. Examples are selling through direct mail, using an independent sales force paid on a commission basis, internet sales, and catalog sales. With this channel, to promote the product and make it visible, you can use network marketing, social media marketing, and host or party-plan sales. Thus, the channel is typically associated with lower overheads than other traditional channels. The advantages of direct selling include the following:

- **Higher margins.** Cutting out all middlemen and selling directly to the customer allows the business to make more profits while offering the customers a lower-priced product. All the costs that are saved from not using middlemen are shared between the business and the customers. Cost savings are realized through savings on broker fees.
- **Swift feedback that enables the customization of products.** Direct selling implies that the business controls all processes in-house, from the manufacturing of the product to the marketing, the sale, and the delivery. This allows direct contact with

the customers in the form of instant feedback during contact points and when issues arise. The business is able to react swiftly using this input to customize the product to more effectively suit the needs of the customer.

- **Personalized service.** If there are key value propositions attached to the product whose realization hinges on how the product is delivered, then direct selling is best. If middlemen do not have the specialist skills needed to assume any of the channel functions, then as a business, you are better off carrying out all the channel functions. Through direct selling, the business is also able to offer personalized demonstrations, which leads to high customer satisfaction rates.

- **Protects reputational risk.** Using middlemen implies giving up control over certain aspects of the business, like service delivery. Keeping everything in-house allows for strictly regulated customer experiences and a tight lid on reputational risk.

Selling Through Intermediaries

This is an indirect channel where products go through intermediaries before they reach the end-user. The more intermediaries involved, the longer the chain is. Advantages that accrue to the business with this approach are:

- **Access to a larger customer base without incurring the costs to attract the customer.**
- **More efficient means of distributing the product.** As a business, you benefit from riding on preexisting channels that have been fully developed by intermediaries.
- **Lower distribution costs.** Trying to reach all target customers through direct selling as a new business may be costly.
- **Logistic support provided by intermediaries may improve the customer experience.**

Dual and Multi-Channel Distribution

This is when a combination of channels is used to get the product to the customers. For example, a business can have retail stores where a product is made available and also have a website where goods can be purchased online. The use of multiple channels can increase customer reach and extend the business's product offering to previously excluded customers, resulting in an increase in sales volume and a larger market share. Issues that need to be managed if a multi-channel distribution is opted for include cannibalization and vertical channel conflict.

The channels used by Google to reach its customers and a typical financial services bank are shown below:

Google Channels	Bank Channels
Google Play	Bank branches
Gmail	ATM
YouTube	Internet
Google Maps	Mobile devices
Chrome OS	Call centers
Google Analytics	

HOW TO CHOOSE WHICH CHANNELS TO USE IN THE BUSINESS MODEL CANVAS

These different channels should be comprehensive and based on market research to determine the best possible distribution channels. To complete this block on the business model canvas, you should ask yourself the following questions:

Which channels are preferred by customers? To maximize value, the best approach when selecting channels is to simply make the product available where the customers prefer to shop. As part of creating value for customers, the product should be made easily accessible to the customers. The easiest way to achieve this is to go where the customers are. For example, if the target customers mostly shop online, the product should be made available online. Failure to do so will make the product less visible compared to that of competitors. Here, you should have the customer segments in mind and ensure that all the segments are catered for in the channels selected.

What channels are my competitors using? This is a critical question as you compete for the same pool of customers with your competitors. Studying the channels already being used can give you a wider market view of what works and the channels preferred by customers.

What are the strengths, weaknesses, opportunities, and threats of each channel? After analyzing the pros and cons of each channel, it is always best to choose the one that best matches your value proposition and strongly advances several business goals. Factors that should be taken into account include the cost and impact on the brand and overall business strategy. For example, opting for direct distribution implies that the business is taking on all the responsibilities that would have been taken on by the middlemen, including the risk of holding stock, documentation for tax records, and higher startup costs. If direct delivery will be done, then the startup costs in this instance will include, in addition to storage facilities, the purchase of delivery trucks. Using a business website for online sales also comes with lots of costs, many of which are recurring as shown below:

- Purchasing a domain name.
- Paying for a secure socket layer (SSL) certificate to encrypt sensitive data to protect customers such as credit card numbers and personal information.
- Website hosting costs.
- Web design costs to make it aesthetically pleasing to customers and mobile-friendly. Responsive web design allows the website to detect the platform that it is being used on. The layout changes to fit the screen of the device it is being used on. This is an

important aspect as customers use various devices and still expect the same functionality.

- Technology to automate operational and financial processes to reduce errors in the purchasing process. As customers shop, they expect to see the total cart balance change, and the website should also accurately calculate taxes due.
- Search engine optimization. This is what makes your products appear in engine search results if customers search for the products that you offer. Businesses that invest in this always rank highest and, as a result, get more visitors on their website.
- Pay-per-click advertising. These are the adverts that you see on web pages when browsing.
- Copywriting. This is money paid to freelance writers to come up with content for web pages.
- Social media. These are costs paid to create social media posts.
- Conversion rate optimization. These are strategies designed to capture potential

customers who visit the website to convert them into paying customers.

A good channel puts the customer first and focuses on the needs of the end-user. Since value propositions also focus on the needs of the user, channels should be a platform on which these value propositions are best delivered to the customer. In summary, end-user needs should always be matched to the channels used by considering the following:

- Personalized service
- Convenience
- Necessity of product customization, installation, or servicing

TROUBLESHOOTING CHANNEL WOES

The business model canvas is not a static board that is only worked on when the business or product is launched. It has to evolve as more information is collected from various sources—research and development, market research, feedback from customers, and an evaluation of how the business is performing. This flexibility allows various aspects that affect value creation to be played around with until a successful formula comprising all the blocks on the business model canvas is crafted. As the business environment is not static, only those businesses that have built-in flexibility succeed. If the product, despite being differentiated from that of competitors is not doing as well as expected, it is worth investigating if the challenge could be emanating from the channels being used. Some telltale signs could be read from the following:

Failure to hit revenue goals: If there is a demand for the product and a product designed to address the specific needs and wants of the customers is available but revenue goals are not being met, then there could be friction points in the distribution channel. A possible reason could be poor information flow—sometimes, target customers do not know where to buy the product or access the service offered.

Difficulties in managing the channels: The distribution channel is, in most cases, the main method in which value propositions are delivered. As such, these channels must be monitored and managed to ensure congruence. Failure to do so will result in customer complaints and bad reviews. If from customer reviews, you discover that customers are not getting the promised value, then the problem could be in the channels being used. Typical example problems that you should be on the lookout for are:

1. Price mismatches. If the product is supposed to be the cheapest in the market, but customers are being asked to pay more than the recommended price, then channel members may be selling at higher prices and reaping off customers.
2. Poor delivery times.
3. Poor service.

Keep in mind that without proper channels, your business model will not achieve the overarching aim of any business, which is to maximize value for the business by delivering value propositions for the customers.

CHAPTER 8: CUSTOMER RELATIONSHIPS

The customer is the most important stakeholder in any business. The business needs customers if it is to kick off, survive, grow, and make a profit, hence the saying "the customer is the king." Customer relationships are, therefore, an indisputable block in the success of any business plan. Customer relationships explain the nature of interaction or association between the business and its customers. This relation is influenced by how the business acquires, retains, and grows these customers. Building strong and winning customer connections is a vital tool to gain a deeper and more intimate understanding of the customers. It also unlocks value for the business as customers can keep coming back and referring others, ultimately building customer loyalty, brand name, and boosting sales.

A business should always strive to create rapport with its customers. It is without a doubt essential that every business has a clear masterplan on how to ensure that they get customers for the business, keep these customers, manage them, and strengthen the customer base. Business startup, survival, growth, and profitability are all interconnected with how the business addresses this important slice in any business model canvas. Several important factors that shape the business-customer relationships have to be paid due consideration. These factors include:

1. The customer segments' expectations on the characteristics of the relationship they wish to have with the business. This is, in turn, shaped by factors such as the contextual environment, the type of customer service offered and expected, and, generally, the actual association.

2. The customer relationships already in existence.

3. The size of the business.

4. The cost of managing and maintaining these interactions.
5. How best to integrate them into the business model.

Customer relationships can crystallize themselves in various routes as personalized service, automated customer service, self-service, and segmentalized service. It is, therefore, important to address the following key aspects regarding customer relationships:

- How do you get customers?
- How do you manage and retain them?
- How do you maintain and grow these customers?

HOW DO YOU GET CUSTOMERS FOR THE BUSINESS?

It is fundamental to always perceive customers as people with values, needs they want fulfilled, and challenges they want addressed as opposed to viewing them as acquiescent recipients. Your product should aim for the fulfillment of the customer needs and expectations as well as to provide solutions to their problems, thus creating value. Full comprehension of the customer will lead to better value creation. Vital considerations that are important when filling in the business model canvas include:

- How will the business get its initial customers?
- How will the target group become aware of the business and its products?
- How do customers evaluate whether to buy the product or not?
- What needs to be done to make that first procurement and to maintain the product after purchasing?

Before attending to these aspects, it is 'mandatory' to answer questions on who these customers are, their thoughts, their vision, their feelings, their activities, and how these affect the business and its products. In short, you should thrive to know your customers —and this includes both the existing and potential customers.

HOW TO CONNECT WITH YOUR PROSPECTIVE CUSTOMERS

Knowing who the targeted customers are is important because customers can be diverse depending on the nature of the business. It is, therefore, always necessary to pinpoint them and consider their diversity and homogeneity. This will aid in the resolution of whether to segment or not to segment the market. Customer segmentation entails categorizing the respective customers into similar groups based on certain uniform features. As discussed in Chapter 6, segmentation can be a function of demographics, geographical location (regional, national, rural, or urban, among others), social factors, and behavioral aspects. Segmenting customers allows for a deeper and closer understanding of who they are, what they consider important, and what solutions they are looking for. This increases the prospects of value addition. In knowing the customer, the following essential matters should be considered:

- **The problem to be addressed.** It is crucial to always start with identifying the problem at hand that your business model will seek to address. It is meaningless to provide a solution to a non-existent problem. The greater the magnitude of a problem, the bigger the chances of customers being more amenable to the solutions that your business seeks to provide. In knowing customers and how to get them, businesses must do market research and feasibility studies and understand the challenges faced by customers and accordingly craft relevant and affordable solutions to these identified challenges.

- **Budgets and customers' willingness to pay for the product.** Questions to be answered here are those such as:
- Are customers prepared to pay for the product?
- Which customer segments are likely to pay the most?
- How much are they willing to pay for the product?
- How much will it cost to adapt to the product?
- Are the customers willing to pay a premium for this customization and how much are they willing to part with?

The more appropriate and problem-focused the solution, the greater the potential of customers willing to purchase the product. Different customer segments might have varying customer needs and expectations. It is vital to consider product flexibility as well as the costs of customizing the product to customer segment expectations.

Accessibility of customers. Concerns to do with the accessibility of customers are important. To get customers on board, one should be sure of the ease or difficulty in reaching them as well as the cost of reaching them. Cost-benefit analysis is pivotal. Considering that the aim of the business is to make a profit, the cost of acquiring a customer must not outweigh the benefit derived from getting the customer. The key is to get the customer at the lowest cost possible. It is also necessary to make a balanced and informed evaluation of customer acquisitions as it might appear to be expensive to get some customers in the short run, but for some strategic reasons or outright profitability, it might prove to be more fruitful in the long run. It can be a "worthwhile sacrifice" to shoulder higher costs now. Take into consideration:

- **The magnitude of the desired market share.**

The target market influences the desired customers, current customers, and prospective customers. A business model canvas should have a clear estimation of the target market share, and feasibility studies must have data to inform the cogency of the forecasts as well as achievability of the set targets. The overall impact on the market share should be adequately evaluated, including the incremental impact, the opportunity cost, and the possible cannibalization of the sales and market share of existing products.

- **Value enhancement and reduction effects.** What is the overall feeling toward this potential market? Will serving it create value? How much value? How does serving these customers impact the business's vision, mission, and core values?

Having done all the above evaluations and identified the ideal customers and customer segments, steps have to be taken on how to get these customers. Decisions have to be made regarding the avenues to be used to acquire the customers. The acquisition can be done through the following platforms:

- Online marketing
- Referrals or the use of current customers to expand the customer base
- Print advertising
- Radio advertising
- Offering free trials

Connect With Your Customers Online

In this dynamic and digitalized world, several ways exist to reach out to customers. The aim is to make your presence as a business known and felt by customers and to advertise the business's products. This digitalized world comes with the advantages of information dissemination and makes it easier to converse with customers. It also comes with disadvantages.

Customers have access to more information and can easily compare the business's products and its other activities toward customer satisfaction with its national, regional, and global competitors. This implies today's businesses have to do more to build and maintain customer relationships than their counterparts yesterday. Globalization and technology have not only stiffened and widened competition but have also brought it to the doorsteps of businesses.

There has been a growing increase in online avenues and social media platforms that can be used by the business to market its products and converse with customers throughout the world. Effective use of these online tools to the business's advantage can make your presence known and felt, make an impression, and leave an unforgettable mark. These platforms include:

- Websites
- Twitter
- Facebook
- WhatsApp
- Business advertising platforms
- Blogs

You should also make the website top class and perhaps use a blog to converse with customers. It is very crucial to make your website appealing, engaging, and addictive to get the customers hooked. Engaging implies a two-way conversation; thus, it is important that the online platform markets and sells the company's image, business reputation, brand name, and products to customers and, at the same time, solicits information on the customer to know them better.

Take time to interact with customers, ask questions to get into the customer's mind, and respond to their questions to gain ground to probe more. More probing allows one to get more information on the background of the customer, their expectations, their views, and their perceptions about the business as well as its products. This information is vital to building worthwhile customer relationships through effective online existence. Customers can also be found through other customers.

Referrals or Through Other Customers

How you relate to your customers is not only essential in creating a strong customer base; it also increases sales and ultimately profits for the company. It is equally an important marketing tool to garner more customers for the business. Loyal and satisfied customers are an important channel to market and distribute products and create value for the business and its various stakeholders who include the creditors, suppliers, customers, shareholders, and providers of capital, among others.

Customers who are satisfied with the business's value propositions as well as its products might be an easy and free resource to market the company and its products. In their satisfaction and excitement, they spread the word to others about the excellent service or good products that the business has offered them.

The amplifying impact of this intentional or unintentional advertising will ensure the brand is sold in a hassle-free and less costly manner. The customers have been indirectly turned into "sales representatives" who are not on the payroll of the company. So, it is always important to remember the twofold impact of customer satisfaction—a loyal customer and a brand ambassador all in one. Since satisfied customers can help market the company's products in a fast and efficient manner, the business model canvas should also address strategies that can be employed to exploit this advantage.

Getting Customers Through Advertising Using Radio, Television, or Print Media and Free Trials

These channels work well to increase product awareness and to get customers to try the product. The major consideration with these approaches is the cost involved. However, customer acquisition is just the first step in getting customers. The business model should also address how to maintain these customers. Therefore, before maintenance, there is a need to outline possible relationships that the business can have with its customers.

FORMS OF BUSINESS-CUSTOMER RELATIONSHIPS IN THE BUSINESS MODEL CANVAS

The best way to build customer connections is through having a full understanding of the customer needs. You can then investigate how addressing these needs and creating relationships with customers affects the compatibility of these relationships with the business model. It is important to ensure that these relationships integrate well with the business model. The evaluation largely leans on two important aspects: the type of service (how personalized?) and the cost of maintaining the relationship (how expensive?).

In a context where customers desire a service that is customized to their needs, it is often costly to maintain such relationships. Customers attach high value to the service, and they usually don't consider it as an enhancement. It is just expected and a non-negotiable part of doing business. Highly customized service will be more ideal for a high-cost business model, whereas it is incompatible with a low-cost business model.

In a low-cost business, high maintenance cost relationships can result in a mismatch between the revenue streams generated and the cost incurred to maintain the relationships. Effectiveness of customer relationships could be another important consideration because, at times, the more effective the relationship is, the lower the costs of maintaining it. Below are some examples of customer relationships that simultaneously exist in businesses:

- Personalized service or concierge test
- Communities
- Co-creation
- Self-service
- Automated services
- Transactional or short term

These customer relationships are briefly explained individually below:

Personalized service. This relationship is largely anchored on human interaction. Customers get personal assistance from dedicated salespersons. In the process, this creates a bond with the company through the representative. Companies can go further to make the relationship a 'dedicated' personalized one. In this case, a customer has a specific salesperson dealing with his or her needs all the time. This creates a unique, deep, and close form of customer relationship. Such types of interactions are found in banks and investment portfolio management companies. Separate bank tellers must be allocated to deal especially with the 'priority' or 'prestige' banking customers, who are normally rich or high-value customers. The business wants to make these customers feel special, give them a hassle-free service, and make money at the same time. In most cases, the account maintenance charged for these accounts is higher than that of ordinary accounts. Some call this section of banking 'premium' banking, implying that there is an extra cost or premium being paid for such dedicated service. From the customer's view, time is money. The customer would rather pay more for dedicated, quick, and efficient service. The same applies to investment portfolio management companies where you can have a stockbroker or investment manager solely positioned to deal with certain clients.

Communities. The word 'community' signifies a sense of working together and building some form of understanding and close-knit ties among members of a group. Taking it in the customer relationship context, it refers to a situation whereby the business establishes a platform, e.g. a Facebook page, through which the company's sales representatives and customers can interact with each other and discuss their experiences as well as knowledge in dealing with the business. The enhancement in technology has opened room for businesses to take advantage of communities to indirectly bring customers under one roof in the comfort of their homes. Communities also allow customers to interact and address each other's challenges. This can be a vital way to strengthen the bonds between the company and its customers and between the community of customers.

Despite this being an effective way to learn more about customer habits, what is important to them, and their views about certain issues, sales representatives must be trained on how to respond to queries on these online platforms. Remember, there is comfort in numbers. Customers can feel more powerful in a community and be aggressive or even outrightly abusive in their engagement with the business representatives on the platform. The salesperson needs to display a great deal of composure, keep emotions under check, and remain as professional as possible in addressing the complaints and queries. The sales representative is the face of the business and must represent it effectively. If he or she promises to get more information on the issue and come back to the client, that must be done in the quickest possible way to instill confidence in the relationship. If not properly managed, the same effort that was meant to create value for the company through building strong relationships might end up destroying value.

Co-creation. Customers are increasingly recognized and incorporated by businesses as much more than just customers but as contributors to value creation. This is especially noticeable in the design of products. The character of the business-customer relationship is greatly becoming dynamic; customers are encouraged to give reviews and ratings on the business and at times asked for their input in designing, redesigning, and innovating products. This creates a strong sense of being valued, ownership, and acceptance of the products. Customers view themselves not just as purchasers of goods who will increase sales for the companies but as stakeholders whose contribution to improving the product is equally important.

Self-service and automated services. In a self-service relationship, the business has no direct interaction with the customers as all the requisite tools are available for the customers to serve themselves. The self-service relationship can be further complemented by automation to upgrade it to an automated one. For example, through the creation of an online channel for customers, the system can pick the relevant features from the profile and use them as a guide to make suggestions to customers on the ideal products for their profile. It can be less costly to maintain the relationship, but it can be time-consuming and expensive to design the appropriate tools to allow for the automated service. It requires proper planning to bring it to functionality.

Transactional and short term. This kind of relationship is once-off and triggered by a transaction. For example, a small grocery at a bus station. Despite the short-term nature of the relationship, it is still important to offer good service because one may never know who the person will tell about the service they received. If the comments are negative, it might negatively affect business reputation.

Having diagnosed the nature of the relationship that the business wants to establish with customers in the business model canvas, the business can now focus on how to keep the relationship(s).

HOW TO KEEP CUSTOMER RELATIONSHIPS

To retain a customer, it is not adequate to just keep them satisfied. Modern-day customers are looking for more in a relationship with the business. Satisfaction is just not enough. Maybe a little more recognition and a sense of ownership of the products and a feeling of being valued can do the trick. Businesses have to go the extra mile. Several methods can help businesses to go above and beyond in their quest to retain customers and build successful relationships. Below are some of the strategies:

- Know and understand your customers
- Ask for and act on feedback
- Show gratitude and appreciation
- Always go the extra mile

Know and understand your customers. Communication is the key to a good and effective customer relationship. Communication is also a two-way process whereby all parties take turns to speak and listen. It is important that while selling the business ideas and products in a well-packaged manner, time is taken to also find out more from the customers, like their views and expectations. That would make one understand what each customer segment values. Is it personalized service? Or do they want the fastest and most efficient way to conduct transactions? Some customers might be very price-sensitive and perhaps purchase more when products are now at the end of range and discounted. Others like to be among the first to own a product. It is important to understand your customer to build the right relationship that meets their expectations. To achieve this, it is crucial to maintain communication with both the current and potential customers. The company can have a clear policy that is documented and communicated to employees on customer handling. Where follow-up is needed, it should be done quickly.

Ask for and act on feedback. It is vital to get feedback from customers, be it favorable or unfavorable. Most businesses have platforms where customers are asked to complete short survey questions while they are being served. For example, in a food establishment, customers can provide this feedback while they wait for orders to be prepared. These short surveys focus on the quality of service and recommendations on how it can be improved. This feedback needs to be taken seriously and accordingly addressed. For example, if it is a compliment (strength), how can you build on this strength and exploit it to your advantage to gain an even greater competitive edge over your competitors? If it's a weakness, how can you turn it into a strength? Always strive to address customers' concerns. Both positive and negative feedback are equally valuable!

Show gratitude or appreciation. It is good to always show care and appreciation to customers. Display genuine care always. Customers might just need to vent or share one or two ideas, and the salesperson must be willing to offer a listening ear. It is also equally important to work with their pace. If they are in a rush and want a short conversation, give them that. Be always true to your brand and its promises. Deliver that which you promise. It is also important to reward customers, and there are a variety of ways to show appreciation. Some use discount programs, and others use loyalty points. In some instances, businesses give away complimentary gifts in the form of branded pens, T-shirts, and hats, among others just to show gratitude. These might seem small, but they are valuable for value creation and a sense of appreciation in the minds of customers.

Always go the extra mile. The business can make an extra effort to keep the customers informed and engaged through things like:

- Outreach programs
- Blogs that keep the customer connected and hooked to the business
- Pop-ups through emails
- Events such as drawings
- Free content to showcase the company's products and brand
- Print media such as monthly newsletters and articles.

After retaining customers, it is prudent to grow them.

HOW TO GROW CUSTOMERS

Customers can be grown in diverse ways. The measures used to retain them can also be used to grow them. These include referrals, next-sell, and cross-sell, among others. Several other strategies can be used to enlarge the customer base. Key among them are the following:

Fully understand the customer as well as the business itself. A deeper understanding of the customer (their goals, aspirations, vision, mission, expectations, and general preferences) enables the business to properly match the needs of the customer with services or goods supplied by the business. Knowing the customer well gives a company a competitive advantage over its customers because its products "hit the bullseye" in meeting the expectation of the customers. If the business products are on point, the business becomes the preferred supplier. It results in a more fruitful interaction as the business works toward customizing its products in exactly the way desired by customers.

The key is to provide the right solution to the problem. For example, for businesses like those in the clothing business, knowing the customers' age and fashion preferences can help the sales representatives know who to inform when they get which kinds of goods in stock. In some cases, the salesperson can set aside something for the customer because they know them well due to the long-term relationship with the company. In that case, the customer base is being grown and the customer feels valued. Smaller businesses also exploit the advantages emanating from their size to offer more personalized services as they can have an in-depth appreciation of the customers' needs. This is an advantage that big businesses don't have. It is vital also to know your business well enough to be able to adapt to customer needs.

Balance your resources and time to serve the existing clients and solicit new ones. Take note of the twofold nature of the broadening of the customer base. Businesses must strive to strike a balance between retaining old clients and bringing new ones on board. The long-standing customers need to be kept satisfied and their morale boosted so that they feel valuable to the company, which invariably leads them to spend more. New relationships have to be sought and nurtured to maturity.

Deliver efficient and unique customer service that makes you stand out from the rest. The best customer service on its own is one of the most crucial strategies to grow a business. Customers spend more time when they feel relaxed and confident in dealing with a business. The first time they might be skeptical and cautious, but as they get assured that they are in good hands, they become more willing to trust the business and spend more. Customer service requires a balancing act, whereby the business consistently evaluates its performance against the needs and expectations of customers and speedily takes corrective measures when value propositions are not delivered as promised or when customers are unhappy over a certain issue. The feedback given personally or through social media platforms must be used as the starting point for corrective action and to continuously improve business processes and the relationship with customers.

Exploit the available networks. Established networks and relationships are known as "social capital" that can be employed by the business to boost its sales and grow its customers. Some businesses get clients through networking. For example, a company contracted to construct houses can refer another company within its networks that provides plumbing services to be considered for engagement to do the plumbing job. The key to broadening the customer base through networking is to deliver excellent customer service and build trust within your networks. This is another way to get referrals.

Partnerships. Partnerships can be another easy way to bring customers under one roof and grow the customer base.

Using social media. Platforms such as the Internet, Twitter, Facebook, and other websites can be used to reach out to a wider range of customers.

SWOT and PESTLE analysis. These can be some of the tools used by businesses to grow the customer base. SWOT analysis can allow the company to take advantage of strength and opportunities to grow the business and customer base to greater heights. Weaknesses and threats can be minimized and worked on to mitigate their impact on the business and avoid a loss of customers. Environmental scanning through evaluating Political, Economic, Social, Technological, Environmental, and Legal (PESTLE) aspects will also assist the business to identify ways to grow customers.

EXAMPLE OF THE CUSTOMER RELATIONS BLOCK

Google attracts and retains its customers by adopting a problem-solving approach. The business value model lists the things that attract customers, retain them, and result in the ever-increasing customer base for Google as shown below:

Customer relationships:

- A fast search engine
- Search results that are relevant and of a high standard
- A simple and user-friendly interface
- Pay-per-click advertising
- Good developer support for android developers

CHAPTER 9: COST STRUCTURE

The cost building block outlines the costs that will accrue to a business depending on the business model that it has chosen. Costs drive a business and are a key consideration in any business. This building block in a business model canvas is largely concerned with mapping key activities to the costs and aligning these costs with the business's value propositions. The determination of the nature of the costs as well as their quantification is largely anchored in how the model expounded on the other fundamental blocks such as key resources, key activities, and key partnerships.

Profitability is a function of the costs and revenues in business. How the costs and revenues are managed has an impact on the survival, growth, and profitability of a business. It is also imperative to identify the business's major cost drivers and link them to revenue streams. The majority of businesses collapse because of the mismatch between revenues and costs or poor analysis of costs that lead to the achievements of the desired value propositions. The inextricable linkage between the costs and cost drivers, value proposition, and long-term sustainability is often poorly evaluated, resulting in negative implications. When the costs incurred exceed the revenues derived, then there is a loss. When the scenario is reversed and revenues exceed costs, this signifies that the business is making a profit and is likely to continue operating and expanding. The surplus profits can be used for reinvestment or diversification into new markets or new products. An extensive assessment of the costs will address key issues such as:

- Type of business in relation to costs
- The nature of the costs commensurate with the business model
- Key resources that are a consequential expense

- Key activities that signify a significant cost
- How these key activities drive the costs
- The link between the costs, activities, and value propositions

TYPE OF BUSINESS IN RELATION TO COSTS

As highlighted above, costs are a major consideration in a business model. Businesses can be primarily classified in terms of these costs. Even though all businesses want to lower costs to increase profits, some businesses strive to have cost reduction as the bare minimum of their mission. Then there are those businesses whose major focus is not the costs per se but how to deliver value.

Cost-driven. It is necessary to distinguish between cost-driven businesses and value-driven ones as the pricing structures will equally differ. Cost-driven businesses tend to have a cost-based pricing structure. Cost reduction is a major concern for this business model. The business seeks to produce at the lowest possible cost. This will influence the structure of the business as it is bound to have a thin cost structure, high levels of automation, and low-priced

value propositions. To minimize financial investments in terms of costs, complex processes could be
addressed through outsourcing. Operational effectiveness and efficiency are key to cost containment
and management. It is key for such a business to
consistently research ways of managing and
decreasing the costs to continuously reduce the
costs. It outpaces competition through producing at
lower costs, thus enabling it to charge lower prices
and attract price-conscious customers.

It is always important to also strike a balance
between cost reduction and the maintenance of
quality because there is often a trade-off. The price
is calculated based on the costs incurred to produce
the product. This includes costs such as design costs,
manufacturing, marketing, and distribution costs.
For a cost-driven business model, the price normally
ranges between lower extremes and higher
extremes. The former is referred to as the "floor
price," signifying it is a starting point toward pricing
a product. The latter is described as the "ceiling
price," suggesting that it is the highest price that can
be acceptable in the market. Businesses price their
products between these two prices to strike a
balance between making a reasonable profit and not

overpricing their goods. The profit margin is determined using the costs as a foundation. Profit margins for cost-driven models are generally lower than those derived from value-driven models, making cost-based prices generally cheaper.

Value-driven. As much as costs matter for any business, some businesses do not largely anchor on cost reduction but on the 'value' they deliver or the one that customers attach and derive from their products. Such businesses are value-centered and require in-depth research into customer segments and their expectations. They also benefit from the analysis of competitor products to see how to deliver value better. The approach is built on designing products of high value that can be priced at a premium to compensate for the price of customizing them to the customer or customer segment's needs and expectations.

For example, a Mercedes-Benz is a high-priced vehicle because customers are willing to pay for the value propositions associated with the vehicle such as the prestige, high speed, comfort, status, and uniqueness, among other valuable features. Providers of the vehicle are equally prepared to incur the necessary costs to deliver those value propositions and accordingly recover the costs through appropriate pricing. The value-based model is often capital intensive because customers want to pay a higher price that is linked to the high value derived from the product. This model has bigger profit margins, though the challenge is that value is difficult to quantify as it is a matter of perception.

The nature of the costs. Cost structures can take different forms, for example, fixed costs, variable costs, and semi-variable costs. The nature of the costs also shapes the way these costs are managed.

Variable costs. From the term 'variable,' these costs vary with output. The more the output, the higher the cost. Production or distribution triggers the costs. In some instances, they can be costs per labor hour. These are driven by demand, for example, if the variable cost of producing one product is $10 and for July, production demand is 2,000 units, the variable costs will be $20,000. Assuming demand increases by 100% in August, variable costs accordingly increase to $40,000 ($10 x 4,000 units).

Fixed costs. Contrary to variable costs that increase in line with an increase in production, demand, or distribution, fixed costs from the term 'fixed' are static. They remain unchanged despite the volume of goods produced. Examples of these are rent, salaries, utility bills, startup, and the cost of acquiring assets. If rent is $10,000 per month, it will remain unchanged despite increases or reductions in production. It can only be changed when it becomes necessary to review the provisions of the lease agreement. Thus, in the short term, fixed costs evidence some form of stability over time.

Operating leverage. The relationship between the variable and fixed costs is explained in terms of operating leverage. It can be used as an indicator to assess a business's future. If fixed operating costs are comparatively higher than variable operating costs, operating leverage is said to be high. On the other hand, if fixed operating costs are smaller than the variable operating costs, operating leverage is said to be low. Considering fixed costs are static and stable over time, higher operating leverage can allow for an increase in profitability in times where the demand for the business's products is high. The fixed costs are spread over many units lowering the cost per unit produced and creating room to make a profit. In times of economic recession, high operating leverage is not desirable as it can lead to a reduction in profits.

Capital and operational costs. Companies budget for and evaluate different costs differently. Costs can be further broken down into capital expenses (CAPEX) and operational expenses (OPEX). The former describes expenditures toward long-term investments, and these are considered under assets in the balance sheet. Examples of these are property, plant, and equipment. For such costs, it is important to do a proper risk-and-return analysis through capital investment appraisal decisions such as payback period, discounted payback period, net present value, and internal rate of return, to name a few. Consider the useful life of the investment, the contribution of the investment, and the expected cash flows. OPEX covers operational costs concerned with the day-to-day expenses of maintaining a business such as electricity, water, repairs and maintenance, and cleaning expenses.

Economies of scale. Costs can also be reduced through economies of scale. This is a cost reduction that accrues due to producing high volumes. As a result, big companies that produce on a mass scale such as the likes of Coca-Cola have, over the years, seen the cost of producing one unit decrease due to efficiency gains. Costs such as fixed costs are spread over high volumes of products. At the same time, the business may also incur lower variable costs. For example, a business can realize a reduction in the raw materials needed, waste, or even the labor hours in the production process due to the synergistic effect or efficiencies in the production process. These efficiencies lead to lower total unit costs. The lower the cost of production, the greater the opportunity to maximize the cost advantage without compromising quality. This allows a business to compete on costs more effectively and price its products lower. These high levels of production silently imply the purchase of bigger volumes of inputs such as raw materials. The high volume of purchasing affords the business a high bargaining power as a customer; they can negotiate for reduced prices through trade discounts. These savings can equally flow to customers in the form of lower prices.

Economies of scope. Cost reductions accruing from economies of scope could emanate from diversification into various markets or a greater breadth of operations. The higher the volume of goods or groups of goods manufactured, the greater the likelihood of a reduction in the average production costs. For example, in the case of adding more products in the product mix or new markets, the company can exploit its long and well-established departments in the launching, marketing, distribution, and selling of the new products or in entering new markets. Functions such as human resources, production, marketing and sales, accounting, or finance that are already in existence can aid expansion and diversification in a way that is manageable, hassle-free, and economic. For diversification in terms of new products, economies of scope are likely to be enjoyed if the new additions on the product mix have similar processes or other commonalities. For example, if a bread manufacturer adds to its product line cakes and donuts, the processes and raw materials are similar.

IDENTIFY KEY RESOURCES THAT CONSTITUTE SIGNIFICANT EXPENSES

As discussed in Chapter 4, key resources are the essential inputs that a business needs to implement a business model. These are the essential resources needed to enable the company to deliver its value propositions, address the customer segment, and supply the product to the customer. They could include things such as raw materials, property, plant and equipment, and the requisite human capital.

For example, the key resources for a beverage manufacturer will differ from those of a clothing manufacturer. These key resources will influence the key activities carried out by a business. The value and superiority of the key resources will affect the survival, competitiveness, and profitability of the business. It is always important to establish whether the key resources, be they human capital, infrastructural, or financial, can achieve the demands of customers. For example, if a company wants to add a new product line or diversify into new markets, the questions in terms of costs and key resources and activities will be: What are our key resources? What will be our key activities? How will these activities influence costs?

Key Activities That Signify a Significant Cost

Key activities are those activities that are essential for companies to undertake to gain a competitive advantage. For example, for a bakery, production and processes to reduce wastage and preserve the freshness of bread considering it is a perishable product will be key activities. Effective distribution channels could be a key resource.

Cost drivers. A cost driver is a reason why a particular cost is incurred. It is the absolute root of a cost and its impact on the total cost incurred. There are several ways to allocate costs using cost driver rates. These include methods like activity-based costing (ABC), standard costing, cost-volume-profit analysis (CVP), and throughput accounting. To identify cost drivers in your business, consider the building blocks from the business model canvas that are closely linked to costs. For example, the key resources and key activities will yield cost drivers.

Activity-based costing. This is a method adopted to allocate both direct and indirect costs more effectively as opposed to the traditional absorption method. It's described as a more accurate and reliable way of distributing costs to a product based on the activities that are undertaken that wholly contribute to the cost of producing a product.

This process requires the business to identify the important costs, determine the key activities that contribute to a cost pool, and calculate and allocate the costs in line with the activity that consumes the resources associated with that cost. An activity is explained as a particular piece of work undertaken with a specified aim. The purpose could be to contribute to the designing of a product, its production, or its distribution, or perhaps it's a process for setting up equipment for production or operating that machinery.

The costs are attributed to individual products or product lines depending on the resources used by the activity. In this case, it is important to establish the major factor that gives rise to a particular cost being incurred, thus the term "cost driver." These cost drivers can be used to analyze the profitability of individual customers or the cash generated by each revenue stream. Therefore, where there is limiting or a constraint on the key resource, resources can be distributed to revenue streams in order of profitability or which one generates more cash. Examples of cost drivers in ABC include machine hours, number of production runs, and labor hours, whereas those in cost accounting include the number of orders delivered, setups, and processed orders.

Despite the preference of ABC as an effective and more accurate way of allocating costs, it has its problems too. It can be complex and time-consuming. In some instances, the costs might be untraceable and difficult to allocate. The other shortcoming is allocating fixed costs in a similar way as variable costs, despite the former being stable and consistent over time and the latter being volatile and fluctuating in relation to the volume of production and change in the constantly evolving business world.

The cost structure block from Google is as follows:

Cost structure

- Investment in research and development
- Software development
- General and administrative costs

CHAPTER 10: REVENUE STREAMS

Businesses are there to fulfill their key objectives and the expectations of various stakeholders. All businesses other than charitable and ecclesiastical organizations aim to make profits and provide a reasonable return to their shareholders (return on investment). The profitability of the business, as well as the cash flows generated, therefore, become important considerations in evaluating a business model.

Profitability is a function of costs and revenue streams. It is important to analyze the anticipated outflows necessary to implement the business model and ultimately deliver value propositions to customers or customer segments. At the same time, the possible revenue streams that can be generated by the business model should also be evaluated.

Revenue streams are described as the cash that originates from a particular customer segment as opposed to the profits arrived by deducting the costs from the revenues. In a business model that is customer anchored, customer relationships are a very important factor in the generation of revenue streams. They help one understand the value propositions valued by the customer segment, the segment's expectations, what they are willing to pay for, and how much they will pay. The costs incurred must be recovered through proper pricing, and these are also informed by the chosen business model, whether it's value-driven or cost-driven. The costs and revenues must equally reflect:

- The business model adopted
- The logic for its adoption
- The forecasted product life cycle

It would not make any economic sense to undertake a business if the cost of designing, creating a product, and delivering it to a customer exceeds the price that the customer is prepared to fork out for the same product. The exception is when this is a market penetration strategy. In this case, the evaluation focuses on the revenues that the product will produce over its life cycle. The product can make losses during the launch phase but rake in more revenue as prices increase during the other stages.

An in-depth revenue stream evaluation is pivotal for any business as this would guide in choosing the appropriate pricing mechanism. A business can have multiple revenue streams defined in terms of the pricing policy adopted on each. For example, the prices could be volume-determined, fixed, or reaching through bargaining, auctioning, or changing market forces. What remains fundamental is the fact that many businesses have failed in their years of infancy. Many others have gone back to the drawing boards to redesign their products or services, seek new customer segments, and revamp their value propositions because revenue streams were poorly estimated in their business models.

WHY IS IT SO IMPORTANT TO HAVE AN UNDERSTANDING OF REVENUE STREAMS?

In performance management, revenue is considered a key performance indicator. Revenues can be used by businesses to evaluate their performance and to situate it in line with the overall business strategy of the business. Revenue is key to the business itself and its various stakeholders. For example, shareholders are interested in when the business will start generating revenues and the magnitude of those revenues to make an informed decision on the return and opportunity cost for the funds. Suppliers, on the other hand, are interested in the business generating enough revenues to sustain itself, grow, and survive. This guarantees the continuity of the business and ensures that the suppliers have steady customers. Bankers, especially when they have supplied capital in the form of a loan or overdraft, will be keen to see whether the business makes adequate revenues to repay the loan and its interest component. So, both the potency of forecasts made and the actual occurrence of these revenue streams are pertinent to the different stakeholders' proper assessment of the viability of the business now and in the future.

DESIGNING A REVENUE MODEL

A revenue model describes the structure outlined by a business as a guideline for producing revenue. It is a master plan or strategy of how business is going to generate revenues. Decisions have to be made regarding the following:

- The products that are going to be offered by the business
- The value the business is going to deliver
- The price at which the product and this value are going to be offered
- Who the customers are and what they are willing to pay for that value

The best way to create an effective revenue model is by making informed forecasts of both costs and revenues. The revenue estimation must be done progressively through the life cycle of the product, taking into cognizance the constantly evolving business environment. What was predicted yesterday might not hold water tomorrow. Continuous forecasting allows for corrective action to remedy any deviations from earlier predictions.

Revenue forecasts are informed by important determinants such as prices of products, anticipated volumes to be sold, discounts, returns inwards, and refunds. In making resolutions on the structure of the business model, a decision has to be made on how the revenue streams would be structured, whether they will be transactional, recurring, or a combination of both. In choosing the appropriate revenue model, the business must consider the following factors among others:

- **Contextual alignment of the model with the business:** Companies often employ different revenue models for varying reasons. Different models of prediction can be used and different processes and procedures employed to estimate the anticipated revenues. Where the revenue streams are repetitive such as subscriptions, the model can display a uniform framework like a template or blueprint in revenue forecasts.

It is important to contextualize the model designs to a given situation. The revenue model adopted must have a strategic fit with the business organization. For example, a business that has a strong technological focus has to have a high budget on research and development as it needs to keep abreast of the changes in technology to remain relevant, deliver value propositions to the customer, and generate adequate revenue streams.

- **The model's ability to maximize value for the business:** The chosen model must be able to enlarge value for the organization. The revenue model must speak to the business model canvas block of costs, depending on whether the business is cost-driven or value-driven. It must be clear what sets the organization as a cut above the rest. Is it the value it delivers or the products delivered at a lower price? How the business meets its stakeholder expectations as derived from the customer relationship is key.

- **The model's propensity to allure appropriate investors:** The revenue model employed must take into consideration its capability in drawing investors to the business. As discussed in Chapter 8, for a business to deliver value, it must start by identifying a problem that it seeks to address. The bigger the problem, the higher the chances of uptake for the solution. It will also be easy to work with investors who are keen on providing the appropriate solution to the problem identified. It also gives credibility to the proposed solution in the eyes of the investors. Investors are interested in making a return on investment from the capital they put in; therefore, timelines regarding the projected cash flows as well as when they are expected are important.

- **The flexibility of the revenue model:** Pliability is an important feature in any revenue model. The digital world often makes revenue models complicated as models can be digital and complex. The generation of revenue is dependent on sales, which are influenced by the ever-changing business world, customer preferences, and industry factors. This shows that the revenue model should ideally be flexible enough to reflect changes that deviate from earlier predictions. This flexibility ensures adaptability so that changes brought about by the continual re-forecasting are incorporated into the model without difficulty.

Factors that shape the variability of revenues must be pinpointed and things that contribute to the various factors such as the product life cycle and other processes identified and planned for in advance. Scenario and sensitivity analysis can be employed in evaluating different scenarios. For example, the following can be taken into account:

1. What if demand increases or decreases?
2. What if operating costs increase?
3. What if the business has resource constraints or a limiting factor?

It is important as part of determining revenue streams for a business model to perform risk analysis and evaluate risks such as political risks, economic risks, exchange rates, and business risks. The business strategy can then include how to identify, manage, and reduce the impact of the risk.

TYPES OF REVENUE STREAMS

There are two major types of revenue streams: transaction-based and recurring.

Transaction-based revenues. Just like the transactional customer relationship, the revenue is produced from a one-time purchase and payment for the service or product. A good example is an ordinary sale. These revenues are not stable over time as they can fluctuate with the increase or decrease in the quantity demanded by customers.

The variations can also be influenced by the change in seasons or consumer tastes and preferences as well as other factors in the external environment.

Recurring revenues. This revenue is generated from repetitive payments being made for the value drawn from the value propositions delivered to the customer or some continuation-after-purchase service offered to the customer. Subscriptions are an example of recurring revenue. They can be paid monthly, quarterly, bi-yearly, or yearly, but all these exhibit recurrences. The repetitive nature of these revenues makes them easily forecasted and estimated with a bit of certainty because of the consistency of cash flows.

DETERMINATION OF THE APPROPRIATE PRICING STRATEGIES

It is always important to identify the right pricing mechanism that recognizes that demand and supply are often a function of the price. The law of demand argues for an inverse relationship between price and demand. An increase in the price of a product results in a decrease in quantity demanded. The choice of pricing strategy will, therefore, influence the magnitude of revenues originating from a revenue stream. Pricing strategies include volume-dependent prices, customer segment focused, and bargaining, among others. These strategies are categorized into two wide groups: the fixed and dynamic categories.

Fixed Pricing

The term 'fixed' suggests stability. The price remains stable and consistent over time because the inputs used in creating and delivering the product remain consistent. Examples under this category are:

- **Customer segment dependent prices:** Having studied and understood the customer segments, the customer relationship they desire, and customer expectations, the business can aim to deliver their customized value propositions at a specific price. The pricing is specifically fixed for this segment of customers that are willing or not willing to pay for certain value propositions.
- **Volume-determined prices:** The quantity bought influences the price at which the product is sold. The higher the volume of goods purchased, the lower the price. In

such cases, the customer is given a trade discount based on the quantity purchased.

- **Fixed-list pricing:** The price is fixed by the manufacturer for the service, product, or the business's value proposition.
- **Product feature anchored pricing:** The product is priced in line with the number of features that it has, especially where it has multiple value propositions that are valuable to the customer.

Dynamic Pricing Strategies

The prices, in this case, are unstable and consistently change. The variability of the prices is closely linked to the variables or inputs that are used to create the product as well as the dynamism of the market conditions. Some of the pricing strategies are as follows:

- **Yield-management pricing:** The price is solely dependent on the inventory and the purchase time. Businesses exploit customer intelligence to generate revenues. During peak times, the price is higher, and when activity is low, the price is correspondingly lower.

- **Bargaining-price determination:** This price is arrived at through negotiation between the buyer and the seller. The price determination could be skewed to the side that wields more power or is more skilled on the negotiation table.
- **Auctioning:** Here, the product goes through a bidding process whereby prospective buyers table offers. These offers quote what the buyers are prepared to pay for the product based on their perceived value of the product. The highest bidder gets the product. In short, the final price of the product is linked to its value in the mind of the buyer.
- **Market-based:** The price is a function of market forces. The levels of supply and demand determine the price. The price rises and falls in relation to demand and availability. Normally, if demand exceeds supply, the price tends to increase, and if supply exceeds demand and the product is abundant in the market, the price falls.

REVENUE STREAMS FOR THE BUSINESS MODEL CANVAS

There are various ways to produce revenue streams. When filling in the business model canvas, the revenue streams that can be included are:

Subscription fees. The revenue stream is recurrent as the customer makes periodic payments for continuity in using the service. For example, professional bodies such as the Chartered Institute of Management Accountants (CIMA) charge yearly subscriptions to members for continued membership so that they continue enjoying the professional services that go with the membership. Many businesses have adopted this kind of approach where they have created databases that can be accessed through yearly, quarterly, or monthly subscriptions. Examples of these are subscriptions to access music, academic articles, and computer games.

Asset sale. An asset can be tangible or intangible. Asset sales generate revenues if the customer purchases the ownership rights of a physical product from the seller.

Leasing revenue streams. This revenue stream originates from the use of an asset. Through a lease agreement, the lessor agrees to grant the lessee an exclusive right for usage of the property for a period agreed upon and stated in the terms of the lease agreement. If the rent to be paid is on a yearly, quarterly, or monthly basis, the lessee makes recurring payments as prescribed. Examples of assets that are normally rented out include franchises, copyrights, cars, and buildings

Usage fees. The revenue streams are determined by the extent of usage of a particular service. The higher the usage, the higher the revenues generated. Examples of such include hotels and service providers for utilities like electricity and telephones. For example, in the case of electricity, the bills are linked to the units consumed. The greater the number of units used in a given month, the higher the payment.

Lending. In the case of loans, the lender sells the right to use his money or capital in exchange for periodic payments in the form of interest. What the lender gets over and above the initial principal amount granted to the client is the revenue stream.

Brokerage fees. This revenue stream accrues to a third party that has acted as a negotiator or intermediary between the buyer and the seller. Good examples of earners of such revenue streams are stockbrokers who bring together buyers and sellers of shares or estate agents who administer properties as well as collect rent on behalf of owners. The stockbroker earns brokerage fees, and the estate agent earns a commission. The revenue streams are recurring in nature. Recruitment agencies, on the other hand, charge a fee for matching a company looking for a candidate with a certain skill with that company.

Advertising. This type of revenue stream emanates from advertising fees that accrue to a business from advertising its brand, service, or product. With the advent of technology, the Internet, and e-commerce avenues, advertising revenues have become a significant revenue stream for most businesses. Companies in various industries—for example, media, software, and other service providers—rely on this type of revenue.

Licensing. Customers are granted the right to use the intellectual property at a fee, thus generating a revenue stream. The owner of intellectual property does not have to incur large capital expenditures in manufacturing the product and making it sellable; instead, they just sell the right to access and use the intellectual property. The technology industry normally has this type of revenue stream, like the right to use software packages like NVIVO for qualitative research analysis. The license expires after the paid-for period ends.

The revenue streams from Google are shown in the diagram below. Note that services that are offered for free are also included in this block.

Revenue streams

- Users get free access to some products like email, maps and the Google Chrome browser
- User payments for advanced features on email
- Payments for website space and keyword auctions
- Licensing
- Subscriptions
- Other offline projects like smart glasses, humanoid robots, and autonomous cars

---

Once you are done with this last block, you have a well-researched, well-documented, and complete business model!

CONCLUSION

Starting a business is very much like building a LEGO house. You start with the foundation, which is the business plan, and then slowly add more to it. If your business fundamentals are solid, like the foundation of a building, your business is more likely to stand tall and be part of the 10% of businesses that succeed. That solid foundation comes from a solid business plan.

This book set out to show you all the components that go into making a business plan. This goal has been accomplished by introducing and breaking down an important strategic management tool: the business model canvas. Using this tool, your business model will become clearer, sharper, and more focused. A properly researched business model helps you become aware of the subtle but important issues embedded in the operating environment. The more you learn about your environment, the more equipped you will be to withstand the vagaries that befall most startups.

Starting a successful business requires passion; commitment; the right mix of technical expertise and business knowledge; a willingness to observe, listen, and learn; and the ability to adjust to market prompts. Is your business idea ready for the market? This ultimately depends on the business plan! After reading this book, you should be equipped to create a comprehensive plan that takes a bird's-eye view of all core issues that you need to take into account for your business to succeed.

Keep in mind that coming up with a business plan involves iterative processes. When coming up with a business plan, print out the business model canvas and hang it up somewhere where you will see it every day. Much like building a LEGO house, sometimes you have to recreate, tweak, and change things. Should the going get hard, do not give up. If, after reading this book, you have to start writing your business model from scratch again, remember that you now have more knowledge than before and can build an even more focused business plan. You have got what it takes it to accomplish this.

Thank you for taking the time to read this book. If you enjoyed it, please consider leaving a review. I would love to hear how your business has been changed for the better.

REFERENCES

Amit, R., & Schoemaker, P. J. (1993). Strategic assets and organizational rent. *Strategic management journal, 14*(1), 33-46.

Booth Partners. (2017, June 7). *5 Tips to Choosing the Right Outsourcing Partner*. Booth & Partners. https://boothandpartners.com/blog/5-tips-choosing-right-outsourcing-partner/

Hayes, A. (2019). *Behind Business Ecosystems*. Investopedia. https://www.investopedia.com/terms/b/business-ecosystem.asp

Laja, P. (2019, May 6). *How to create a unique value proposition (with examples)*. CLX.Org. https://cxl.com/blog/value-proposition-examples-how-to-create/

Lumen Learning. (2008). *Marketing Channels in the Supply Chain | Boundless Marketing.* Lumenlearning.-Com. https://courses.lumenlearning.com/boundless-marketing/chapter/marketing-channels-in-the-supply-chain/

Outsourcing Law Global. (n.d.). *What and When You Should Not Outsource | Outsourcing Law.* Www.Outsourcing-Law.Com. Retrieved June 23, 2020, from http://www.outsourcing-law.com/what-and-when-you-should-not-outsource/

Stillman, J. (2016, April 14). *No Office, No Problem: 125 Companies Proving That Virtual Companies Can Thrive.* Inc.Com. https://www.inc.com/jessica-stillman/no-office-no-problem-125-companies-proving-that-virtual-companies-can-thrive.html

Strategyzer. (2019). *How do I use the Customer Segments building block of the Business Model Canvas? – Have a question? Find the answer here.* Uservoice.Com. https://strategyzer.uservoice.com/knowledge-base/articles/1194379-how-do-i-use-the-customer-segments-building-block

The Monash University. (n.d.). *Marketing dictionary.* Monash Business School. Retrieved June 29, 2020, from https://www.monash.edu/business/marketing/marketing-dictionary/

Ulman, Z. (2020, February 20). *Council Post: 5 Things To Know About The Affordable Housing Crisis*. Forbes. https://www.forbes.com/sites/forbesrealestate-council/2020/02/14/5-things-to-know-about-the-affordable-housing-crisis/#253916bb48a0

Valamis. (n.d.). *What is Knowledge Management? its Importance and Benefits*. Valamis. Retrieved June 24, 2020, from https://valamis.com/hub/knowledge-management

Made in the USA
Las Vegas, NV
18 February 2024

85961010R00121